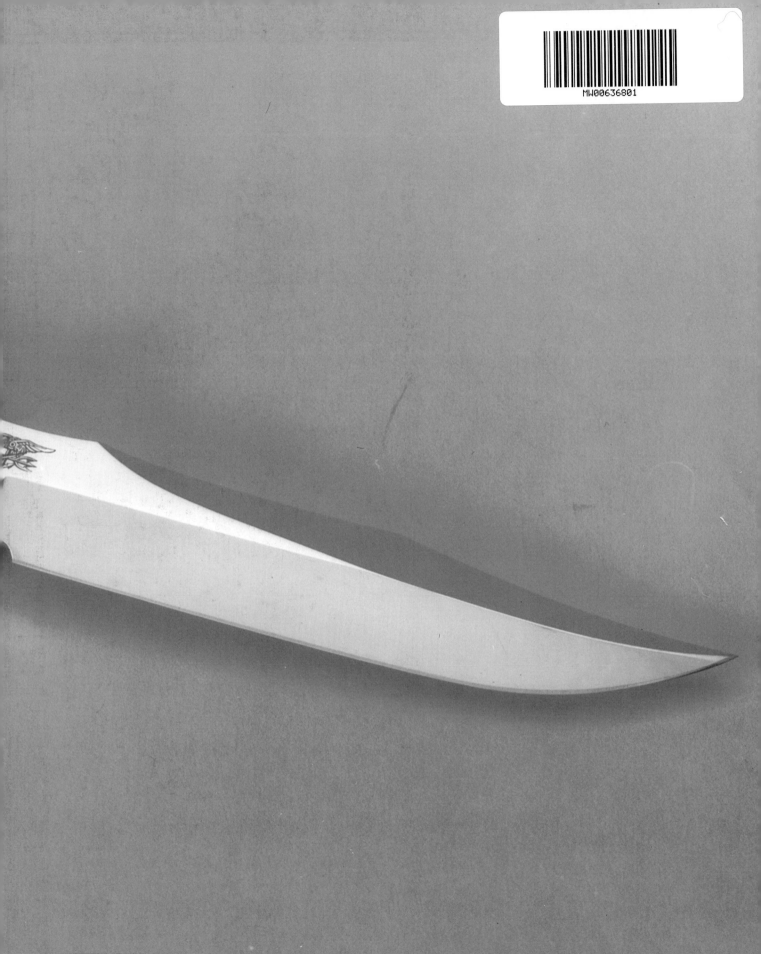

MODERN
COMBAT BLADES
THE BEST IN EDGED WEAPONRY

DUNCAN LONG

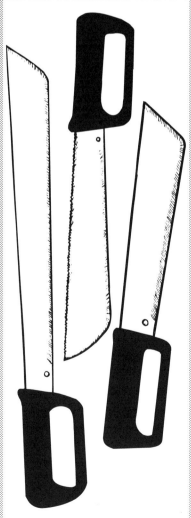
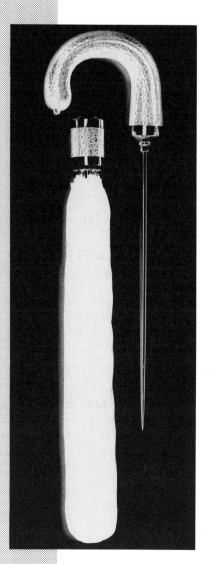

PALADIN PRESS • BOULDER, COLORADO

Also by Duncan Long:

AK47: The Complete Kalashnikov Family of Assault Rifles
AR-7 Super Systems
The AR-15/M16: A Practical Guide
AR-15/M16 Super Systems
Automatics: Fast Firepower, Tactical Superiority
Combat Ammo of the 21st Century
Combat Revolvers: The Best (and Worst) Modern Wheelguns
Combat Rifles of the 21st Century: Futuristic Firearms for Tomorrow's Battlefields
Making Your AR-15 into a Legal Pistol
The Mini-14: The Plinker, Hunter, Assault, and Everything Else Rifle
Mini-14 Super Systems
Modern Ballistic Armor: Clothing, Bomb Blankets, Shields, Vehicle Protection . . .
    Everything You Need to Know
Modern Sniper Rifles
The Poor Man's Fort Knox: Home Security with Inexpensive Safes
Powerhouse Pistols: The Colt 1911 and Browning Hi-Power Sourcebook
The Ruger .22 Automatic Pistol: Standard/Mark I/Mark II Series
Streetsweepers: The Complete Book of Combat Shotguns
The Sturm, Ruger 10/22 Rifle and .44 Magnum Carbine
The Terrifying Three: Uzi, Ingram, and Intratec Weapons Families

Modern Combat Blades:
The Best in Edged Weaponry
by Duncan Long

Copyright © 1992 by Duncan Long

ISBN 0-87364-670-3
Printed in the United States of America

Published by Paladin Press, a division of
Paladin Enterprises, Inc., P.O. Box 1307,
Boulder, Colorado 80306, USA.
(303) 443-7250

Direct inquires and/or orders to the above address.

CONTENTS

WARNING

Technical data presented here, particularly technical data on combat and self-defense, as well as the use and alteration of edged weapons, inevitably reflects the author's beliefs and experiences with particular equipment and bladed tools under specific circumstances which the reader cannot duplicate exactly. The information in this book should therefore be used for guidance only and approached with great caution. Neither the author nor the publisher assumes any responsibility for the use or misuse of information contained in this book. It is *for information purposes only.*

ACKNOWLEDGMENTS

*T*hanks must go to the many companies and manufacturers who were especially helpful in supplying sample knives, bayonets, swords, machetes, hatchets, and other edged instruments included in this book, as well as photos, drawings, and other information contained herein. Among those who must be singled out for offering advice and information, and in many cases for sending out sample products, are: Spencer Frazer, SOG Specialty Knives; Toni Zona, Camillus; Gary T. Randall, Randall Made Knives; Mike Boisvert and Max Yablonovitch, Y.B. Technology; Sherilyn Trippany, Century International Arms; Al Mar, Al Mar Knives; Kellen C. Greene, Atlanta Cutlery; Charles Ebersole, Catoctin Cutlery; Rosemarie Finnegan, Sportsman's Guide; and Tom Jahn, Spyderco, Inc.

Assistance was also extended by master editor and knife expert Ken Warner, who generously gave copies of his *Knife Digest* to the author through the years.

Thanks should also be given to Peder Lund, Jon Ford, and the other fine people at Paladin Press for producing this book. Paladin Press goes out of its way to help writers—something that can't be said about all publishers.

And, of course, my customary special thanks to Maggie, Kristen, and Nicholas for their continued patience with the crotchety writer who lives with them and loves them all very much.

INTRODUCTION

*E*dged weapons date back to prehistoric times. They generally were tools of stone (primarily flint) and fire-hardened, sharpened sticks and horns utilized as crude stabbing weapons. The Bronze Age (spanning 1500-1100 B.C.) saw the creation of bronze knives and swords, which served their owners from Crete to Britain. These were gradually displaced by iron during the first millennium B.C., when the secret of smelting iron ore spread from Asia to Europe. Styria (Austria) became the source of the best iron ore and quickly became the center for blade production.

During the Middle Ages, the cities of Innsbruck and Passau became known for their exceptional iron blades. Though tempering was known, these blades weren't nearly as hard as modern irons and bent easily until the Vikings revolutionized the process with the introduction of carbonized iron.

As in ancient times, today's cutlery industries are centered in several key spots of the globe. They ship their products to various distributors, create special designs for dealers, and even sell parts to custom bladesmiths. The best known of these manufacturing centers are Solingen, West Germany; Seki City, Japan; Sheffield, England; Thiers, France; and to some extent the New England region of the United States.

Many of today's combat blades being produced by manufacturers and custom smiths have changed very little in concept from those first flaked-flint knives employed to thwart raiders dressed in animal skins or dispatch savage animals, a somewhat surprising fact in light of modern firearms capable of "picking off" opponents at ranges of hundreds of yards with ease. With serious talk of hand-held laser weapons being available in the near future, edged weapons might seem sadly outdated or even obsolete.

But they aren't. If anything, there probably are more types and greater numbers of edged weapons designed for combat floating around today than in any other time in history. Part of the reason for this is simply that there are more people today. With more people alive now than have died in the past, it isn't hard to see that the numbers of most types of weapons are greater now than in any time previously. This isn't the whole reason, however. A more important point is that edged weapons are the most versatile weapons ever devised for close-quarter fighting.

Edged weapons are not like firearms, which can expend their ammunition quickly; and a gun without cartridges becomes a useless paperweight or, at best, an awkward club. A knife (or battle ax or other bladed weapon), on the other hand, is always ready to draw blood. A bladed weapon never jams, doesn't require reloading, and is always ready even if it's been submerged in water for hours or has lain in web gear for months at a stretch. Mechanically, a blade is about as simple as a tool gets, making it tougher and longer lasting than more complex weapons like firearms. Furthermore, where firearms are complex to manufacture, almost anyone can take a piece of flat steel and create a utilitarian knife with the simplest of home tools or even coarse rocks suitable for grinding an edge on steel.

Firearms are not always ideal for close-quarter fighting when opponents are within grappling range. In such a situation, a firearm becomes hard to aim, is easily deflected or snatched by an enemy, and may even pose a danger to the person wielding it should an adversary lock his arms around the shooter. Firearms are, in reality, more offensive than defensive in many ways.

Not so with edged weapons.

Within fifteen feet, a man with an ax, sword, or dagger can actually close the distance between himself and a man armed with a firearm *before* the firearm can be brought into play. It's possible for a skilled combatant wielding a bladed weapon to dispatch a gunner without being injured (a fact more than a few people carrying a firearm have discovered the hard way).

Edged weapons are more flexible in how they're used during an attack and can often be utilized for more mundane jobs as well. For example, a knife can be used to open a can of beans, cut a tent stake, or skin game. A battle ax or machete can cut firewood, and the former can be employed as a hammer. Furthermore, most bladed weapons can actually create crude secondary weapons. Stakes sharpened by a bladed weapon can be used as punji sticks in highly effective booby traps or on crude spears. By way of contrast, firearms are useful only for actual combat, sporting endeavors, and perhaps for gathering game—*if* the caliber isn't too powerful for the animal being hunted.

This is why most soldiers from ancient times to the present have carried a knife of one form or another. Today, a combat knife—often in the guise of a bayonet—can be found at the side of almost any trooper anywhere in the world when he's outfitted and ready for duty. Many infantrymen will even have *several* bladed weapons on their persons, and not a few airplane pilots and naval personnel will have a knife of some sort "just in case."

Of course the edged weapon is no longer the king of the battlefield, but in many ways, neither are small arms. Modern warfare has become mechanized and somewhat automated. An enemy is engaged at ranges of miles by aircraft and artillery. As opposing sides close, machine guns, grenades, and mortars bathe the battlefield with shrapnel and bullets. A soldier is either dead or hidden in a trench or behind safe cover before he gets close enough to utilize a bladed weapon. Only during moments when enemies stumble into each other (often in darkness) do bladed weapons prove to be important assets on most battlefields. Then they may be essential for survival.

The more cynical will suggest another reason why bladed weapons aren't considered important to military strategists: they require skill to use. Practice and attention to improving skills are essential if a person is to attain the ability to wield a knife or other bladed weapon to its full advantage. With the average soldier not being enthusiastic about obtaining fighting skills (a fact that's often surprising to those outside the military) and with most armies having neither the time nor the resources to give recruits the months of training that mastery of bladed weapons requires, it isn't surprising that only elite troops have much skill with these specialized weapons.

For civilians, the situation is totally different. Recent restrictive gun laws have disarmed many citizens (though not the criminal population). This has forced the law-abiding to search for alternate tools suitable for self-defense as crime continues to grow despite—or even because of—ill-conceived firearms regulations. While many knives have also been outlawed, especially in urban areas, the wide variety of bladed tools and little-known variants of bladed weapons usually enables citizens to stay one step ahead of legislators intent on disarming the public. Furthermore, inexpensive weapons are hard to trace and cheap enough to discard, making it possible for citizens to "walk away" from a crime scene with little fear of being connected to the crime or prosecuted for defending themselves.

All of this has led to a growing interest among civilians in everything from "decorator swords" (which can be pulled off the wall to cut "unexpected visitors" to size in the dead of night) to plastic "letter openers" and "ice scrapers" that can be utilized to seriously wound any mugger unfortunate enough to pick on an armed "victim."

Economics also come into play with edged weapons. While many collector's knives and custom-made bladed weapons are very expensive, modern manufacturing methods coupled with new alloys and plastics have reduced the price on other combat tools. Where most firearms suitable for combat cost hundreds of dollars, plastic daggers, sharpened screwdrivers, and other self-defense tools covered in this book are available for just a few bucks. Many feel that this has the added benefit of making these edged weapons easy and inexpensive to replace; the theft or confiscation of such a weapon becomes almost inconsequential to an owner.

Another economic factor in bladed weapon manufacture is the growing collector's community and reenactment groups. These two markets have created enough demand that anyone wanting a weapon nearly identical to those carried by Julius Caesar's troops or the knights of old can simply purchase one, no

questions asked, for a small sum. Likewise, durable blades created to the purchaser's specifications by custom knife makers from steels only dreamed of in the past are available in many cities and accessible to all corners of the world via the mail. And again, the cost for these masterpieces is small.

(It should be noted that this explosion of designs, ranging from ancient to ultramodern, makes covering all varieties of edged weapons in a book like this impossible. Therefore, this manual will concentrate on the more important and mass-produced varieties within each category and direct the reader to the best sources of these and similar weapons, as well as reference books giving more detailed coverage of the diversity of designs now available.)

Most citizens find that combat blades have another advantage over firearms and other types of weapons. Because of the enormous number of bladed weapons, it's nearly impossible to legislate these "tools" away or trace them to their owners. Unlike guns, which have serial numbers and thus paper trails that can lead government workers right to the doorsteps of legal owners (though not necessarily to criminal owners), bladed weapons are "clean."

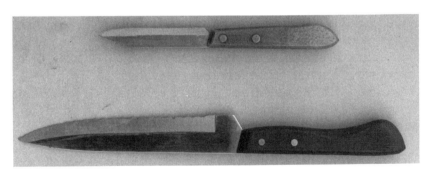

Knives are common tools, and the huge numbers that have been manufactured combined with their ease of fabrication make it impossible for repressive governments to truly disarm citizens.

As history has shown time and again, weapons with paper trails allow government bureaucracies to quickly confiscate such devices "in order to protect the public."

While the purpose of this book is not to present an antilegislator diatribe, history is full of examples of restrictive governments attempting to disarm the law-abiding and criminal alike. Unfortunately, many well-meaning laws succeed only in disarming those who obey the law, often creating more victims in the process. Most criminals continue to carry the weapons, and those formerly law-abiding citizens not willing to give up the restricted devices become criminals by breaking the law. This has been demonstrated time and again by the continued use of knives and firearms in countries and areas with restrictive laws—as exemplified in Washington, D.C., among other places. (Those wishing to get a good overview of how complex the legal system pertaining to edged weapons has become should read James R. Nielsen's *Knives and the Law*, available from Knife World Publications.)

Of course, laws notwithstanding, there will never come a time when all the steak knives, ice picks, and screwdrivers in a country will be confiscated, even by the very worst of Big Brother governments backed up by "thought police." There are just too many edged weapons around, and the ease of fabricating "low-tech" knives and daggers enables anyone with two hands and a file or grinding wheel to make a knife from scrap metal in a matter of hours.

For those interested in legal arguments, there is also the in-vogue-again/out-of-vogue-again theory that each man has a natural right to defend himself. Common sense seems to dictate this to most rational people, man-made laws to the contrary. The late science fiction writer Robert Heinlein once wrote that an armed man is a free man. Certainly elite troops who have been trained to handle a knife, as well as those citizens forced to exploit a blade for self-defense, have discovered that edged weapons offer this added feeling of self-assurance and freedom.

This self-confidence is reflected in a manner and body language that will often cause criminals to avoid attacking such a person rather than discover the hard way *why* a person has such self-confidence. Being armed doesn't mean a person should take unnecessary chances, but it does enable him to continue his daily routine in a less fearful manner and with fewer restrictions to his movements. Should a criminal decide to assault an armed citizen, this self-confidence can often provide the added edge needed to prevail during the fight. In effect, an edged weapon can give its trained owner courage when he would otherwise be scared spitless!

On the receiving end of things, edged weapons have a high psychological deterrent effect on many would-be attackers. While a weapon should never be presented unless the person holding it is serious about using it, sometimes just the sight of a wicked-looking blade will be enough to cause a foe to surrender or decide he has more pressing business elsewhere. The blunt fact is, most people are more fearful of a knife attack (and especially of an attack with an ax or short sword) than they are of being shot.

If a bladed weapon must be used in combat, it can be used quietly and efficiently. This enables citizens to defend themselves from criminals without creating unwanted attention and, once the defense has been mounted successfully, quietly "melt away" after the fighting is over. In many areas, this is an important plus that keeps innocent citizens out of jail. (While self-defense is a natural right, legislation to the contrary often makes it risky to exercise this right. Consequently, in areas of the world where bureaucrats have made life dangerous, the quiet efficiency of bladed weapons is an important plus that enables many victims of crime to avoid becoming victims of the state as well.)

This silence can sometimes be important on the battlefield as well. Combat knifes are more quiet than even "silenced" firearms (which often are far from silent), making them ideal for dealing with sentries or for close combat in areas where overwhelming numbers of enemy troops may be in the vicinity.

So whether a person is an inner-city citizen trying to protect the few possessions he owns or a soldier on the modern battlefield, a combat blade of one sort or another is often found at the side of those facing trouble.

It's a safe bet that citizens of the next few centuries will continue to carry weapons concealed upon their persons. While many of these weapons may be constructed of newer alloys and plastic (with the latter being capable of avoiding ever more common metal detectors), they'll likely be nearly identical in size and shape to those carried in seventeenth-century Italian courts or on the streets of eighteenth-century London. Likewise, if there are ever any "starship troopers" in the future, they'll undoubtedly be toting some type of bladed instrument—not unlike that utilized by their twentieth-century counterparts.

• • • • •

Combat blades have been intertwined with mankind's survival from ancient times to the present. There's little doubt that this will continue well into the future as these simple but efficient tools provide self-defense for citizens and soldiers of future civilizations.

Chapter 1

OF MYTHS AND TACTICS

There's a wealth of misleading information—if not outright myths—concerning edged weapons. Not a little exaggeration can be found in books, magazines, and movies where knives and other weapons in the hands of villain and hero alike are capable of tasks far beyond reality. These often make for great entertainment. But such exploits should not be taken into account when you're choosing the best edged weapon for your purposes or trying to develop tactics for your chosen combat blade. *Your first task when choosing a bladed weapon and learning how to defend yourself is to forget most of what you've heard secondhand or seen in the movies.* Take everything with a grain of salt.

Needless to say, believing myths about bladed weapons can be dangerous. On a personal level, fighters may freeze up when an enemy, stabbed by a blade, fails to drop dead on the spot or even show any sign that he realizes he's been injured. Standing with your mouth open is a good way to get killed by an angry, wounded aggressor.

On a national level, some authorities feel that Japanese ground fighting during World War II was hampered by the samurai doctrine held by many imperial officers. This doctrine led to tactics dependent on "banzai" charges that required maneuvering troops within bayonet and sword range of their enemy. Since Allied troops were armed with semiautomatic and automatic weapons, huge slaughters of Japanese soldiers often occurred as they strived to get close enough to use their bladed weapons. The Allies' tactics of staying under cover and massing firepower on the enemy proved to be superior to lunging with steel.

As noted in the Introduction, while bladed weapons do have a place in civilian self-defense encounters as well as in the hands of elite troops on special missions, the combat blade has become nearly obsolete as a weapon on today's battlefield. In fact, it's not farfetched to say that bladed weapons have been outdated since the introduction of cartridge-fed weapons.

This is proven by eyewitness accounts of both the Crimean War and

American Civil War. Observers and doctors who witnessed these massive campaigns remarked how bayonet wounds rarely were seen, despite the fact that bayonets often were mounted on the rifles of both sides. Seasoned troops even threw their bayonets away since the tools were simpy deadweight to be carried but never used. (Pro-bayonet authorities argue that bayonet wounds more often are fatal and therefore aren't as apt to be seen by doctors. This idea has not, however, been proven and remains more a matter of faith than fact for those intent on arming soldiers with knives capable of being mounted on a rifle's barrel.)

The rare utilization of bladed weapons in combat is also borne out by a quick study of American casualties during World Wars I and II. During the First World War (which included close-combat trench warfare), the U.S. Army hospitalized slightly more than 224,000 troops with wounds of all types. Of these, 235—less than one-tenth of one percent—were bayonet wounds. Saber (and possibly knife) wounds accounted for twelve hospital beds during the entire war. British percentages for wounds suffered during this war were similar. (And some of these wounds may have been self-inflicted or accidentally caused by friendly troops!) While novels and movies portray the First World War as a time of bayonet and trench knife clashes, the numbers suggest otherwise; shotguns, clubs, and pistols were more often the "trench weapons" of choice.

In World War II, Americans suffered nearly 600,000 battle injuries. Of these, only 1,617 were caused by "instruments or objects, cutting or piercing"—a classification that undoubtedly included sharpened sticks or nails in booby traps as well as knives, bayonets, and swords. This translates to roughly 0.0027 percent—even though Americans in the Pacific faced the Japanese, whose doctrine stressed tactical use of bladed weapons!

Bayonets and knives may have seen limited use in Korea, where American troops occasionally suffered from supply line problems. But by the Vietnam War, use of the bayonet *mounted on a rifle* had become almost unknown. Brigadier General S.L.A. Marshal wrote in the May/June issue of *Infantry* that the bayonet was never used as a bayonet in Vietnam, and while combat knives like the Randall were popular for the hand-to-hand combat that occasionally took place after nightfall in Vietnam, the number of actual casualties from such encounters was quite meager.

It's possible to argue that, in the hands of more skilled troops, bladed weapons take a more substantial toll. This is most likely so with the U.S. Army Special Forces, Delta Force troops, British SAS, and similar groups. Certainly this is true with the Gurkhas, who've based much of their tradition on their *kukri* knives (which are more like short swords than combat knives). But with the advent of breech reloadable rifles, if not earlier, bayonets, knives, and swords became obsolete as far as actual infantry combat was concerned.

In the civilian arena, it's a completely different story.

One reason for this is that most bladed-weapon encounters take place at close quarters. Firearms—involved in criminal/civilian encounters only about half the time—usually have considerably less firepower than is normally seen on the battlefield. Shootings almost always take place within 30 feet and often at arm's length. Furthermore, law-abiding citizens are greatly limited in the types of weapons they can employ. Calling in an air strike on a local street gang—while an appealing idea—isn't an option. And in more intellectually backward areas, gun ownership may be all but denied to law-abiding citizens.

So the percentage of bladed weapons being used by citizens and criminals alike is quite high and, in many areas of the United States, hospitals admit as many or more people injured with knife lacerations than with gunshot wounds. This often comes as a surprise to people who have been led by the media to believe that most crimes involve the use of firearms. This misinformation, coupled with the widespread use of bayonets and knives by soldiers on the "silver screen," has given people a false view of bladed weapons. They are led to believe that combat blades are used more often on the battlefield and guns more often on city streets when, in fact, the reverse is more likely to be the case.

Combat blade designs often enjoy popularity more from romantic stories rather than reality. Heaven only knows how many "ninja" swords have been sold to those impressed with the capabilities of these weapons in the recent onslaught of martial arts movies. Likewise, the legendary exploits of Jim Bowie, Rambo, and various Hollywood heroes have made massive knives (often only vaguely resembling the knife actually used in real life or on the screen) popular.

In fact, these weapons are often less than ideal. The single-edged blade of most bowie knives (which the Rambo survival knives are loosely designed around) limits the ability to slash due to the fact that the forward edge of the blade is sharpened. The symmetrical grip configuration of many of these knives makes it hard to orient the forward edge in the dark, creating greater problems at night. And since knives are designed for slashing attacks, they tend to be big and heavy—and slow. So they aren't for everyone.

(In the case of the "First Blood" knives with their formidable saw-toothed spines, one might argue that they aren't for anyone. The teeth can get tangled in clothing or flesh during combat, forcing the user to stay within arm's reach of his opponent or let go of his weapon. Such designs are far from first choice for self-defense.)

The bowie design—without teeth—isn't all bad, of course, and the bowie knife is a favorite of many seasoned pros. The basic design is strong, and the heavy blade is ideal for cutting (though much the same can be said for a machete, which costs a fraction of the price). This makes such designs ideal for many of the more mundane tasks soldiers and campers often use their knives for and is the main reason the bowie design is used on many modern military, hunting, and survival knives. But the bowie knife is not the magic weapon many think it is, and it does require special tactics when employed against an opponent (as will be discussed in Chapter 4).

The old Mark I trench knife used by American troops during World War I is another example of legend overtaking the truth. The Mark I has a narrow dagger blade with a knuck-

le bow for "dusting" an enemy within arm's reach. It looks very deadly and is easily manufactured. But in actual combat, the thin blade had a habit of breaking off at the tang and, if this didn't happen, the end of the blade often snapped off when it was used for something as strenuous as opening a can of beans. Adding insult to injury was the fact that the "brass knuck" made it hard to maintain a proper grip on the Mark I during a fight.

The legendary Fairbairn-Sykes fighting knife sometimes didn't fare much better, despite the fact that it was issued to various commando-type units in Britain, Canada, and the United States. During World War II, the blades on these knives were poorly tempered and often broke off at the tang or point (especially when wartime production made quantity important and less time was spent heat-treating the blades).

The grip of the Fairbairn-Sykes tends to slip from a wet or sweaty hand, and its round shape makes it hard to determine how the blade is oriented in darkness. So these knives aren't the be all and end all many think, either.

Switchblade knives have also gotten a reputation for somehow being more dangerous than they really are. Part of this status is, perhaps, because of their "forbidden fruit" quality created by the U.S. federal law that essentially outlawed these knives for civilians since 1958.

But switchblades don't really have any features that aren't found in more easily obtained folders (as we'll see in Chapter 3), many of which can be opened as quickly as a switchblade. Switchblades are not capable of being brought into play any faster than regular knives, are not more deadly, and are often unreliable because of mechanisms that wear out quickly or rust easily. And even the best are prone to jamming due to lint or corrosion. Yet switchblades have taken on mythical proportions thanks to the U.S. Congress and Hollywood.

The idea of throwing a bladed weapon in combat is another myth that has been perpetuated in fiction and film. Thrown knives offer more penetration than hand-held attacks because the blade picks up greater momentum when moving at a faster speed. But getting this greater energy on target is hard; precise knife throwing is an art requiring extended practice and a known distance from the thrower to the target to succeed. Most knives are inaccurate when thrown and often are damaged in the process. "Throwing knives," therefore, are usually more suited to circus acts than combat.

The Oriental "throwing star" is another bladed weapon that is often chosen for combat by the less well-informed. Certainly these can pack a wallop if thrown properly and if they strike their intended target (two points not guaranteed by any means). But by and large, throwing stars lack the weight to do more than minor damage with hits to most parts of the body. (As will be discussed in Chapter 11, there are some types of bladed weapons that have been designed specifically for throwing, but these should always be treated as auxiliary weapons since, if the thrower misses his target, he is otherwise defenseless against a counterattack.)

Seasoned fighters don't ever use tactics that entail throwing their primary combat blade. Darts, throwing knives, or throwing stars are treated as tools for harassment rather than deadly devices. Primary weapons are always held in reserve in case the thrown weapon fails.

Just as combat blades have been hyped and their abilities distorted by tall tales and battle anecdotes, the various styles of fighting with edged weapons have been garbled and perverted by proponents of the styles and the stories of their exploits. Unfortunately, some of these styles of fighting can get the novice killed.

Perhaps the worst of these is the "fencing" style of fighting with short-bladed knives. This style is often seen in Hollywood productions (especially in the past) and has been championed by some well-intentioned instructors as well (including John Styers, who advocates a similar system of fighting in his book, *Cold Steel*).

The fencing style of knife fighting reached its apex in 1935 when A.J. Drexel Biddle began teaching his techniques to U.S. Marines and the FBI. Later, Biddle wrote *Do or Die*, which outlined his gentlemanly style based upon fencing techniques suited to sword fighting.

This system is still seen from time to time, despite its dismal failure in real combat, with students taught to shuffle their feet as they weld a 4-inch knife like a 24-inch sword. Unfortunately for anyone using this style, the hand holding the knife is extended in front of the body, allowing an opponent to readily grasp or attack the knife hand. The bottom line: fencing styles should be used only with long-bladed, sword-like weapons.

By the beginning of World War II, Biddle was being laughed off the stage during his demonstrations with marine recruits, who often managed to poke him with their blunt knives during demonstrations of his techniques. Biddle was finally removed from training troops as it became obvious that his style of fighting wouldn't work in actual combat. At this point, more reliable knife fighting methods developed by Capt. E.A. Sykes, Capt. W.E. Fairbairn, and Col. Rex Applegate replaced Biddle's system.

There is a wide variety of fighting styles that do work. While outside the scope of this book, there's a wealth of material in print for those wanting to learn how to fight properly with edged weapons. For those employing knives for defense, John Sanchez's *Slash and Thrust* and *Blade Master*, Don Pentecost's *Put 'em Down, Take 'em Out!*, and Marc "Animal" MacYoung's *Knives, Knife Fighting, and Related Hassles* are all excellent starting points (all three are available from Paladin Press). *Modern American Fighting Knives* (from Unique Publications) by Robert S. McKay also contains a wealth of information. Those interested in Oriental weapons, swords, medieval-style axes, or the like generally can find a wealth of information on these subjects at a large public library. Many will also be able to find martial arts courses in cities (with the caveat to beware of phony instructors teaching fantasy techniques); likewise, many colleges have fencing teams that can at least give a good idea of what can be achieved with a long-bladed weapon.

For those who have studied any of the various Oriental/American styles of unarmed combat, push daggers (also known as "push dirks" or "push knives") are ideal for augmenting these fighting styles *without* having to learn a second technique since the bladed weapon can be employed within many of these styles of fighting. As we'll see later, the push dagger generally is underrated, and some high-quality versions with a variety of blade configurations are now available for those wishing to follow this route.

Once the reader settles on an edged weapon that best suits his needs, he will need to practice extensively to master the device. The target/training methods outlined in Sanchez's *Blade Master* can be readily adapted to any type of bladed weapon and make a good starting place for the novice.

Fighting with a bladed weapon demands greater physical skills than shooting a gun. Those wishing to defend themselves with a modern combat blade should start a realistic exercise course to augment their fighting techniques. No one should fool himself into thinking that sweat and work aren't necessary to master an edged weapon. Fighting with a knife or its more exotic relatives is akin to riding a bicycle or learning to swim. A person can read all kinds of books and know endless "stuff" about fighting with an edged weapon, but until he actually practices and succeeds, he'll never master the essentials he'll need to prevail in an actual hand-to-hand encounter.

Oddly enough, the tactics employed in defense with an edged weapon are best decided *before* the selection of a combat blade. This is an important point; if the novice simply adopts a combat knife because it looks neat or a favorite Hollywood hero used it effectively in the last adventure movie, he is likely to be saddled with a fighting style that won't give him full advantage or be to his liking.

Often this is obvious. A sword or battle ax, for example, isn't going to be ideal for someone looking for an easily concealed weapon to carry on a subway or street in a crime-infested neighborhood. A sword cane is going to be conspicuous on someone built like a weight lifter with no hint of a limp.

But even with nearly identical weapons, the best type of defense mounted will often be determined by the weapon's blade. For example, a double-edged dagger is designed principally for a stabbing attack; a bowie knife, mainly for slashing (even though its single edge limits its capabilities). The dagger calls for closing to grappling distance with an antagonist while the bowie is more ideally suited for an attack near the outside limit of the user's reach.

Likewise, many daggers are almost impossible to utilize as makeshift hatchets, so those wanting a defensive weapon to carry on the trail will probably want to leave an expensive dagger behind and carry a bowie knife, which is ideal for many mundane chores like cutting rope or kindling for a campfire. Conversely, daggers are more convenient for concealment in street clothing than are immense bowies.

Sharp blades are essential for slashing attacks; this usually dictates a wide, probably single-edged blade that can give a deep cut. Thrusting attacks—which give a longer reach to the user and therefore may have an advantage—require a narrow blade capable of penetrating quickly without becoming trapped in an opponent or his clothing. While ice-pick-type weapons work well for this, a dagger blade with a double edge is capable of doing more damage to quickly disable an opponent.

Those wanting to disable an opponent with one heavy blow should choose a heavier weapon like a broadsword, ax, or machete (realizing that none of these are concealable). Again, the right weapon will improve the chances of success and even augment a fighter's abilities, while the wrong choice will hinder him.

The type of hold used to grip a weapon will also determine to some extent the type of handle that will be most comfortable with it. For example, the "natural" or "hammer" hold is the one normally adopted by many (including some skilled knife fighters, despite what some book authors may lead readers to believe). This hold usually dictates an asymmetrical shape on the knife, machete, or ax handle, often with a swelled area under the little finger to keep the weapon from slipping from the hand. The hammer grip is especially ideal for heavy or long-bladed weapons such as battle axes or machetes.

The two-handed hammer hold is suited for those wielding a heavy weapon or who need to maximize their power (perhaps due to a physical handicap). This hold is best suited to Oriental-style short swords and axes that will accommodate a two-hand hold (though some fighters can adopt a hand-around-hand hold that enables them to use a two-hand grip on weapons having a standard hilt).

"Fencing" holds of various styles are another popular way to grasp many bladed weapons. These holds are similar to each other, with minor changes in finger placement between "saber," "foil," and "rapier" styles. These date back centuries and can't be used with many edged weapons like push daggers. But the holds are common with daggers and, of course, swords.

The saber hold is most common and places the thumb parallel with the back edge (or one of the edges) of the weapon, with the fingers spread somewhat along the grip. This hold dictates a more or less rounded grip on a weapon. The saber hold allows both thrusts and slashes and, when used properly, lends itself to a variety of attacks and styles of fighting.

The other most popular fencing hold is the "complete" or "quarter saber," which places the thumb parallel to the flat side of the blade, dictating a slab-sided grip on a weapon. Like the standard saber hold, the complete gives an extra bit of reach, which can compensate for those having a short reach or who are saddled with a short-bladed knife for self-defense. The downside of the complete hold is that it gives a weaker grasp on the grip due to the placement of the thumb.

For some time, the "ice pick" hold was viewed by experts as a "slob hold" adopted by those knowing little about fighting. That's changed, however, with Oriental fighting styles that include a backhand, upper slash to the hold. This hold also permits a downward attack (not as easily blocked as some martial arts instructors have led people to believe) that can't be executed with most other holds.

The ice pick hold generally works best with daggers having double-edged blades and rounded grips. It should be noted that this hold also allows a long-bladed knife to be concealed behind the back and arm quite easily while still in the user's hand, ready for immediate use. On the flip side, the ice pick hold gives the shortest reach of any of the holds and dictates a fighting style many may find alien to their natural fighting tendencies.

Your physical strength will also determine how effective or ineffective a bladed weapon may be. Those wanting to use a heavy, medieval-style two-handed sword or battle ax to defend their home or apartment had better have lots of upper torso strength and arms like a weight lifter's, and a bowie with a 14-inch blade is best suited to the Arnold Schwartzeneggers of the world. By the same token, push daggers or the new "high-tech" plastic knives would be ideal for those not so physically inclined.

The physical limitations of your environment must be considered as well. An apartment with 8-foot ceilings is going to be nearly impossible to defend with any weapon having a blade longer than 10 inches or so since an overhead slash will likely embed a *bolo* or short sword in the ceiling! Narrow hallways or rooms packed with furniture demand short blades and, if possible, jabbing tactics rather than slashing attacks.

Those wanting to mount an attack with a sword—or defend themselves with fancy footwork—can do so *if* they utilize a long-bladed, lightweight weapon designed for jabbing attacks. While the idea of countering an attack with duelinglike parries and footwork is unrealistic (unless both attacker and defender are armed with similar weapons—doubtful in this day and age), a bladed weapon with a pointed blade of 18 inches or longer can be deadly (remembering that more than one "Jim Bowie" displaying fancy thrusts and slashes with an 18-inch knife has been slain by a punk with a shiv who knew how to get in close to administer the coup de grace).

It's also important to avoid edged weapons created more for collectors or display than for combat. As will be discussed in subsequent chapters, the grips on many such knives are not suited for actual combat and can be dangerous to the person holding the knife during the violent impact when the blade makes contact with a flesh-and-blood target.

While the camouflaged grip found on some combat knives is seldom needed, some thought should be given to the finish of the blade on weapons that will be used outdoors. A brightly polished blades can act like a mirror to betray

Modern Combat Blades: The Best in Edged Weaponry

the user's presence for miles. Dull or parkerized finishes on such weapons are a good idea in many cases.

A few edged weapons are poorly suited to combat due to grips with pointed pommels (often passed off as "skull crushers") or cross guards with sharp points or edges that may cause serious injuries to the hand of the person using them. Other edged weapons may lack sufficient cross guards to keep fingers from leaving the grip during a heavy thrust (which becomes a real possibility if your hands become wet or bloody); a defender's fingers can be severely cut on his own blade. So those choosing a combat blade must be sure to keep an eye out for such potential shortcomings.

Some cross guards—as well as grips or hilts—make it impossible to feel the orientation of a bladed weapon without looking at it or touching the blade. Not only can the inability to tell the orientation of the blade by feel slow down the user—perhaps disastrously—it can also mean that the blade will be oriented incorrectly during an actual attack. The most glaring example of such shortcomings is with single-edged knives having symmetrical handles. A confusing fight in poor light can leave the person clutching such a knife with the sharpened edge on the tail of his cutting strokes, causing an enemy to suffer scrapes rather than cuts. The user of such a knife is at a cruel disadvantage during a fight.

Finally, poor design often leaves edged weapons with eye-pleasing projections or shapes that are detrimental in combat. The most glaring examples are brass-knuckle handles of battle axes and knife grips, and blades with saw-toothed edges (whose teeth can get snagged in an opponent's clothing or skin). Less obvious are push daggers, bowies, or stilettos with too-narrow tangs (which have a tendency to snap in combat), tangs that don't extend the full length of the grip, or blades weakened by deep lightening cuts or points that are too long. Such designs can quickly hamstring a fighter who has placed his confidence in the wicked look of his chosen weapon rather than in its actual capabilities.

Some edged weapons being sold for self-defense are so poorly constructed they'll come apart during an attack. Some have blades that snap off during an attack. Others have cutting edges that can fold back to cut the user's fingers. Weapons like these nearly guarantee defeat during combat, so it's essential that a buyer examine carefully any blade he'll be staking his life on. In actual combat, there are no time-outs when a weapon breaks!

Finally, some thought needs to be given to maintaining a bladed weapon to prevent it from being damaged, keeping it sharp for maximum effectiveness, and carrying or storing it when it's not in actual use. The best, most expensive blade can quickly be ruined by rust or corrosion, and a dull edge makes a fine cutting tool behave like a cheap lump of plastic. A knife that can't be removed from its holder quickly or a sword in a locked display case is not going to be ready for combat at an instant's notice—which is all the time its owner may have to prepare to defend himself.

With all the above in mind, here are a few of the positive points to look for when shopping for a combat blade after deciding which fighting style and tactics best suit you:

1) The weapon should be practical to carry or have close by, where it may be needed for defense. If it's being kept in a car or home, it should be easy to reach yet readily concealed from casual viewing (unless it's being used for a wall decoration—a useful ploy in some situations). If the owner must have the weapon on his person, then it should be as lightweight as possible, comfortable to carry, and encased in a sheath that protects it and the wearer while not hampering a "quick draw."

2) The weapon should be affordable and give plenty of combat potential for each dollar spent on it. For most, this means avoiding an expensive, handmade knife. Generally, a mass-produced blade will suit a user just as well, and it can be altered easily with a file or other common tool to suit the user *better* than many custom knives would. Low initial price tags make such alterations less abhorrent to the owner, too, so they are more likely to be carried out. Generally, if the combat blade seems too expensive, it probably is.

3) The grip of the weapon should be sufficiently strong to survive any thrust or blow

delivered with it. This means a knife or sword *must* have a full tang (the metal running from the blade into the handle or grip). This generally can be determined by careful inspection.

With battle axes and similar weapons, the handle or shaft must be of quality wood, plastic, or metal. Using the weapon as a pry bar can quickly determine if it's strong enough, but be prepared to trash a poorly made blade or grip. Bladed weapons made of exotic materials such as modern plastics should be tested carefully to determine how strong they really are; brittle plastics or ceramics that have a tendency to shatter make poor material for combat blades.

4) The blade should be durable. Stainless steel is the easiest material to maintain, especially in humid areas, but is also a bit harder to sharpen. Generally, forged carbon and 400-series stainless steel are the most ideal materials for edged weapons, although new alloys and other materials becoming available may change this.

5) Grips or other "furniture" on a bladed weapon must be durable. The various micartas and plastics are ideal both from strength and maintenance standpoints, though stainless steel or natural wood can be more appropriate for some applications. Stag and wrapped cord handles tend to be less than ideal under many conditions and, in areas with harsh environments, may not last too long. Leather handles should be avoided, as they deteriorate over time, and the salts in the leather may attack the steel of the blade.

Skeletonized grips (which actually are just unsharpened extensions of the blade's tang) should *not* have holes large enough to allow fingers to enter them. Otherwise a finger may slip into a hole and either break during a thrust or cause the hold to become awkward.

6) The shape of the grip should conform to the owner's hand and feel comfortable and natural when the weapon is grasped. The best shape will be determined in part by the hold used as well as the size of the hand. There is no one-size-fits-all handle. A combat blade shouldn't be purchased without first being held to see how it feels in the hand.

7) With knives and swords, the cross guard (also called a "guard" or "quillon," depending on the weapon and maker) should *not* allow the fingers to creep forward after a heavy strike at a target. Subhilts or "knuckle duster" finger guards are best avoided; those desiring these features should be sure they do not overly restrict finger movement or trap the hand in the weapon should it get entangled during combat.

The cross guard should not have any sharp projections that might injure the owner or get entangled in clothing. It only needs to be wide enough to keep the fingers from sliding forward onto the blade. Unless a user expects to duel a foe with a sword (very doubtful), overly wide cross guards, bell guards, or the like are not needed and add only useless weight.

8) With single-edge blades, the handle or cross guard should give a positive indication of how the blade is oriented, even in darkness. With some knives, one side of the cross guard can be bent upward or downward to achieve this end. The handle should have grooves, finger swells, or an oversized pommel to allow the weapon to be retained even if it becomes wet, oily, or bloody. Slick grips should be avoided if possible (though grips can be roughened or modified with a file or sandpaper if the weapon is otherwise ideal). Full finger swells may make it nearly impossible or very impractical to utilize some grip styles.

9) Lanyard holes should be lined for extra strength *if* they will be used.

10) Most people find grips with an oval cross section the most comfortable to use. Handles with a round cross section are suitable on daggers or with fencing holds. Squared-off cross-sectional handles are often very uncomfortable.

11) "Skull crusher" pommels with spikes or similar sharp projections are best avoided since they're likely to injure the user during a fight should his palm come into contact with them or should he strike himself with them when "winding up" to deliver a blow. Flat metal pommels will be nearly as effective in dealing with an enemy and allow the weapon to double as a hammer in a pinch.

12) Heavy-bladed weapons such as machetes, swords, or axes should have an extra-big swell at the end of the grip, a pommel larger than the grip, or a finger guard that wraps around the

grip. This will enable the user to retain the weapon even if his hand gets tired or sweaty. Lack of these features will often cause the weapon to slip from the hand during use—an embarrassment during gentlemanly combat and a disaster in life-or-death encounters.

13) "Blood grooves" are unnecessary, though they can lighten the overall weight of a blade. Lighter weight is better achieved by narrowing the blade. This has the added benefit of creating a more compact weapon that has less friction when shoved into an opponent, making it less apt to become lodged in a wound.

14) Sawteeth on blades are also less than ideal. The teeth tend to get caught in the body of an opponent. Furthermore, most sawteeth on knives are not racked properly to allow them to cut wood; material can be whittled away with a sharpened edge faster than it can be sawed with these knives. All in all, sawteeth are a fad that's better avoided on a combat weapon. (Teeth can be ground off if a weapon is otherwise suitable for the buyer's purposes.)

16) With knives and swords, the "choil" (the area of the blade just ahead of the cross guard) should *not* be sharpened; this will help protect the user's fingers as well as accommodate some specialized types of holds. The choil is usually a bit narrower than the sharpened edge of the blade purely for aesthetic reasons; offbeat designs and some "Arkansas toothpicks" have choils the same width as the blade without any degradation in effectiveness. With broadswords or similar weapons, the choil may have a secondary cross guard above it to allow for two-handed grips.

17) With knives, maximum blade width is generally best kept to 1 1/2 to 2 inches and the length of the blade from 4 to 10 inches (a 3-inch blade may be dictated by legal considerations in some districts). The blade should be thin enough to hold a good edge but thick enough to avoid breaking during any "intensive" work. Swords, machetes, axes, and similar instruments being utilized in rooms with low ceilings should have overall lengths under

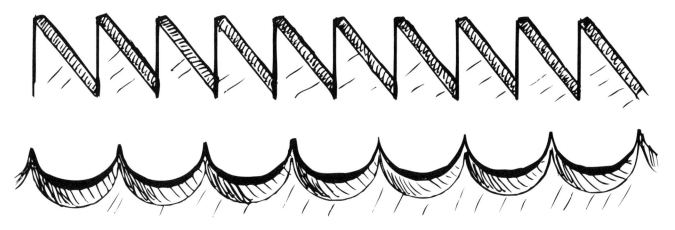

Sawteeth (top) are not ideal on a knife since they can snag in flesh and often cut less effectively than a sharp edge. A serrated edge is another story; it actually improves the slashing capability of a blade.

15) Serrated edges *can* greatly improve the slashing and cutting qualities of many blades. These surfaces are hard to sharpen, however, so anyone purchasing such a blade should be prepared to spend extra time and effort or purchase special whetstones for sharpening it. "Kris," "fire," or "fiamma" blades, which have wavering edges, also add efficiency to slashing. These designs are also easier to keep sharpened.

24 inches. Those using épeé-type swords principally in jabbing attacks will find full-length blades of 36 inches or more will work well even in areas with low ceilings.

18) Wire-cutter holes in blades enable some combat knives and bayonets to be coupled with their sheaths to create a crude wire cutter. These weapons shouldn't be discounted because of this feature, but it is more gimmick than useful since it's necessary to remove the

sheath from the belt (or go through strange acrobatics) to actually cut wire with such a tool. The cutting ability of these bayonets and knives isn't all that great either; only the thinnest of wire can be cut, and the process will dull or damage a small section of the blade as well. If a user needs to cut wire, he's better off buying some real wire cutters!

19) Finally, a buyer should consider how federal, local, and state laws apply to the bladed weapon he's considering. For example, some states allow a person to carry any folder with a 4-inch or shorter blade, while federal law as well as some state and local ordinances restrict blade length to 3 inches or less—and ban all blades from commercial aircraft. Conse-quently, a person could legally carry a 4-inch folder in one place and walk into a federal building, enter an airport boarding area, or cross a state line and be arrested for carrying a concealed weapon.

To discover what laws are "on the books," the knife owner should contact his city and state attorney's offices and determine the facts. Salesmen, friends, and local police officers generally have a poor grasp of the law. (If possible, the "okay" from the attorney's office should be in writing so a photocopy of the letter can be carried in a wallet. This way, if stopped, the owner of the weapon can produce the document and save himself a lot of legal hassles and possibly some time in the holding tank.)

Chapter 2

BAYONETS AND MILITARY COMBAT KNIVES

As noted previously, the bayonet has only rarely seen action in battle during the twentieth century. It seems likely that it will be dispensed with completely in the twenty-first century or, as is the case with the current U.S. Army bayonet, simply become a good utility knife with bayonet attachments for use in parades or morale-building exercises.

This hasn't always been true. The bayonet was deadly effective when first introduced by the British and French in 1660. Firearms were crude at that time, and riflemen needed backup weapons capable of reaching a man on horseback or carrying a pike. The need to reach so far dictated that the first bayonets be long, pointed knives that could be plugged into the bore of infantry muskets, since it was impossible to quickly reload the crude muzzleloaders of the day.

Since the plug bayonet made it impossible to fire a loaded musket (and probably caused more than a few explosions when guns were fired with the bayonet in place), it was replaced toward the end of the eighteenth century by the socket bayonet, which fit around the muzzle, allowing a soldier to shoot even with the bayonet mounted.

In actual combat, a bayonet has a very narrow design parameter in which it will function well. To keep from becoming enmeshed in a foe, a bayonet must have a narrow cross section; a wide bowie-style blade, especially if longer than 4 to 6 inches, creates enough friction during a forward thrust to wedge itself in a human body. This leaves the fighter with the choice of abandoning his rifle and bayonet with his (hopefully dying) foe or firing a cartridge to blow the victim off the end of the bayonet. (The latter maneuver is a dubious proposition at best since, if the weapon is loaded in the first place, it seems doubtful that the fighter wouldn't have fired the rifle rather than use the bayonet.)

Because close-quarter fighting generally offers little room for fancy footwork, the blade needs to be rather short. Additionally, the bayonet can't be overly heavy on the end of the rifle or it will cause the bullet impact to shift according to whether or not the bayonet is mounted. Also, a heavy bayonet will make the rifle slow to bring into play, defeating the whole purpose of mounting it on the rifle for hand-to-hand combat.

What this boils down to is this: about the only truly effective modern bayonet for combat is a short spike. But since most armies don't expect their troops to be fighting with bayonets, a combat or utility knife design is normally adopted so the soldier can use his bayonet as a camp tool or a hand-held battle knife if he needs to do so. Consequently, except for the Chinese military and a few Third World countries that still issue their rifles with an SKS-style spike bayonet, bayonets suitable for combat are nearly nonexistent in today's armies.

Oddly enough, while most of the bayonets now carried by soldiers would perform poorly as bayonets, many are excellent combat knives. And since they are mass produced with an eye to both their effectiveness and their cost, many make excellent buys for civilians searching for a quality combat blade at a reasonable price.

Because bayonets must be capable of being attached to a rifle's barrel, some type of latching system is found on them. Unfortunately, some attachment systems make the bayonet uncomfortable to the hand and, with some, the thumb is actually in danger of slipping into the open ring on the cross guard ahead of the grip. In such cases, the purchaser may wish to weld or silver-solder a plate over the hole and grind or file off parts of the mount clip. For those less inclined to do-it-yourself modifications, it is often possible to purchase nearly the same blade in its "combat knife" form, identical to the bayonet sans attachment assemblies. (One good source of these is Sherwood International.)

In 1884, Sir Richard F. Burton wrote in *The Book of the Sword* (available from Dover Publications), ". . . the precious saw-bayonet, a theoretical *multum in parvo* equally useless for flesh and [gathering] fuel." Unfortunately, the sawtooth seems to reappear on bayonets and combat knives every other generation as new military designers toy with ways to add more utilitarian capabilities to their weapons. While the attempt is noble, as with wire-cut-

ting capabilities, it creates a second-rate tool at best and can cause injuries to those trying to use the blade for a task it isn't up to. And whatever such cutting teeth can do, the sharpened edge of the blade can do better, safer, and faster.

Those searching for a combat blade shouldn't be tempted to purchase a bayonet or combat knife with sawteeth. If they do, they are well advised to grind them flat so they won't get entangled in a foe or his clothing if the owner is forced to use the blade in combat.

Scalloped or serrated blades are another story. While similar in concept to sawteeth, these thinned, toothlike sections quickly cut though material by increasing the angle of the blade slicing through it. Additionally, because they have no opening between sections of the blade, scallops aren't plagued with fouling or getting entangled in whatever is being cut. Consequently, scalloped blades are a plus where open sawteeth are a liability. Hopefully, as automated techniques become more common in knife-making circles, scalloped blades will totally replace saw-toothed edges.

Whether bayonets or combat knives, military blades have two distinct designs which a potential buyer should be aware of. One is designed for dagger-style combat with thrusting attacks; the blade is narrow and the point is at the center of its tip. This design is quickest to bring into play since no "winding up" is necessary (as is the case with slashing attacks), and the distance covered between the attacker and foe is more or less a straight line (as opposed to a curved line with a slashing attack). While the greater speed may not make a difference in most confrontations, a fraction of a second may be vitally important. Therefore, combatants should consider carefully before dismissing the double-edged dagger designs of combat knives and bayonets.

The shortcoming of the dagger design is that the edges have a steeper angle (dictated by the need for both sides of the blade to be sharpened). This makes the cutting ability of a dagger inferior to that of the wide, single-edged blade on bowie-style knives designed principally for slashing attacks. While a dagger, even with a minimal edge, can inflict serious wounds with slashing attacks, it won't be quickly disabling. Therefore, this type of blade dictates a stabbing or lunging style of attack aimed at vital organs, since the blade will often be ineffective at severing veins and arteries in the extremities.

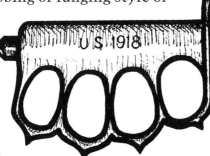
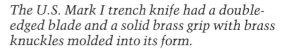

The U.S. Mark I trench knife had a double-edged blade and a solid brass grip with brass knuckles molded into its form.

Among the first of the dagger-style combat knives to see use in the hands of American troops during World War I was the Model 1917 trench knife, which was little more than a 9-inch spike with a grip surrounded by a D-shaped knuckle bow. This was followed by the Mark I trench knife, which was similar in concept but had a double-edged blade and a solid brass grip with brass knuckles molded into its form.

Both weapons were undoubtedly effective, although the awkwardness of the grips dictated by the knuckle assemblies makes them less than ideal by today's standards. Despite these drawbacks, not a few patents, experimental variations, and actual knives were built around these two patterns for U.S. troops, and a few

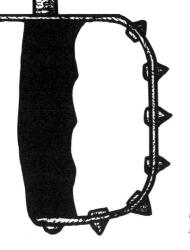

American troops during World War I used the Model 1917 trench knife, a 9-inch spike with a grip surrounded by a "D" knuckle bow.

were carried by American troops during World War II. (For a closer look at the wide variety of these and other designs that never became popular, the reader is directed to M.H. Cole's *U.S. Military Knives, Bayonets & Machetes*, Book IV, available from the author at the address listed in Appendix B.)

The bowie-style blade will accommodate lunging and stabbing attacks, but the thickness of the blade creates greater friction in entering flesh, making withdrawal slower and giving a foe a chance to grapple or counterattack while the owner of the knife is trying to recover from his attack. Many bowies are made heavier in order to achieve better cutting abilities; this works well, but also prolongs recovery time and makes the already slow slashing attack even more sluggish.

Nevertheless, many prefer a wide-bladed bowie-style knife for the simple reason that it has a sharper blade and can therefore handle more mundane cutting chores. It should be noted that a larger bowie-style knife can create disabling slashing wounds to the arms or legs; this allows attacks to be carried out from a distance and may actually be superior in terms of reach and speed *if* a foe is being attacked head-on. So while the shorter dagger is quick and ideal for surprise attacks, the heavier bowie may have an edge once a hand-to-hand fight begins. (Modern armies generally carry bayonets and knives with blades no longer than 7 or 8 inches. However, bowie knives approaching sword proportions are offered on the open market and are popular with civilians. These will be covered in Chapter 4.)

While modern armies have opted for minimal lengths on their combat blades, manufacturers often offer similar models with blades 3 to 4 inches longer for those soldiers and civilians wanting an added advantage. Most notable of these is A. Eickhorn, whose bayonets and knives are imported from Germany and offered in the United States by Sherwood International.

Both the bowie and dagger styles of combat knifes and bayonets have been popular with the U.S. military since World War II. The most famous of the bowie styles is the Ka-Bar. While Camillus actually produced the first knives of this design in 1942, the first of these knives issued to the U.S. Marines was made slightly later by Union Cutlery under their Ka-Bar trade name. This latter name stuck, and the knives continue to be known as Ka-Bars, even though the company bearing the name has since gone out of business. Since that time at least eight American companies have made this knife at one time or another, and more than a few copies have been created in Japan, France, Italy, and Mexico. The Israeli military (which has earned a reputation for no-nonsense selection of issue weapons) has its own version of the Ka-Bar.

With all these variations on the basic Ka-Bar design, one would expect that variations on the name of the knife abound, and this is certainly the case. Among the more common are "K-Bar" and "Kabar." The name itself is becoming somewhat generic, with a lower-case k ("kabar") often seen in print.

The design of the original 1942 knife that became the Ka-Bar was actually based on the navy's Mark I utility knife, the most notable difference being the extension and enlargement of the Ka-Bar's blade. The Ka-Bar was officially adopted by the U.S. Marines as the Mark II, and was often found in the hands of other branches of the military during the Second World War.

The Ka-Bar originally had a round cross-section grip (newer versions have an oval cross section), thin cross guards, and a short, sharpened false edge (so-called

because it is a second edge on an otherwise single-edged blade design) on the spine of its bowie-style 7-inch blade. While this blade has little to offer over similar knives, its thickness coupled with its rugged design make it an excellent utility knife and have much to do with its good reputation. This design has proven to be very popular with American troops and was much sought after by U.S. Army personnel during the Vietnam War. It continues to be carried by American soldiers, who often purchase this inexpensive knife with their own money.

The Ka-Bar design has proven to be popular with American troops and was much sought after by soldiers during the Vietnam War. It is still carried by U.S. troops.

Unfortunately, most Ka-Bars are equipped with leather handles, making them less than ideal in humid areas where the leather may rot and the steel next to it rust. However many military versions of the knife have had the leather treated to minimize rot problems. These are far superior to the Ka-Bars created for civilian sales, which often lack such chemical treatment.

During the Vietnam War, the Ka-Bar design was adapted to work as a bayonet on the M16 rifle. These were only experimental, however, and were finally rejected in favor of the M7. The few remaining examples of these bayonets are available from SARCO.

Camillus has supplied the U.S. military with the majority of its Ka-Bars, and the Camillus version is the most common of the many varieties of the Ka-Bar. At the end of the 1980s, however, Camillus lost its contract with the U.S. government, being underbid by Ontario Cutlery, which now produces the blades for the marines. The early production Ontario Cutlery blades departed from the original Ka-Bar design, with thinner tips that undoubt-

Modern Combat Blades: The Best in Edged Weaponry

edly were more ideal for jabbing attacks but also broke more easily—a major shortcoming for a knife that served more time as a camp tool than a weapon. Consequently, the Ontario Cutlery knives currently being produced are made with the original wider blade tip.

New versions of the Ontario Cutlery knife are also offered with a short saw-toothed spine—a leap backward for this otherwise good design (this can be remedied with a grinding wheel if a standard blade isn't available, however). The Ka-Bar as well as its numerous look-alike copies are available from many suppliers. Among the best is the version from Brigade Quartermasters, reasonably priced in the $25 to $40 range, depending on the model. (Please note that all prices quoted in this book were current at the time of publication.)

The U.S. Air Force/Army Survival Knife (designed to be carried by pilots) combines the basic features of the Ka-Bar with a shorter 5-inch blade and a sheath containing a sharpening stone. While this knife certainly will function well as a fighting weapon, its short blade makes it a second choice for such use.

(For those selecting this knife or others having a sheath for a sharpening stone, one trick suggested by Ken Warner in his

Knives '92 book is to remove the stone and replace it with a small Swiss Army knife or other folding knife. This allows the user to have access to a variety of blades, from his large sheath knife to the smaller folding blades, so he can handle a variety of tasks. For those wanting a "work" or survival knife that can serve double duty as a fighting knife, this would be an ideal way to create a lot of flexibility with "off-the-shelf" components.)

The Ka-Bar's influence is also seen in the French Foreign Legion's knife, which combines a Ka-Bar-style handle with a wide, 7-inch, double-edged blade. This creates a handy weapon

that's ideal for thrusting attacks, with a blade that's thick enough to resist the breakage that plagues narrower blades.

Interestingly, the U.S. Army adopted the bowie/Ka-Bar blade layout for its new M9 bayonet (for the M16 rifle) in 1987. The M9 MPBS (Multi-Purpose Bayonet System) was created by the Phrobis III company for the U.S. military trials and was selected over entries submitted by Eickhorn (a German manufacturer), Imperial (United States), Marto (Spain), Royal Ordnance (Britain), and S-Tron (United States). The U.S. Marines espoused the identical knife, but with a black, rather than green, grip and a plastic sheath. The big pluses of this bayonet are that its blade is stainless steel and it has a plastic handle rather than leather. These features, coupled with the "zone heat treating" of the blade, make the M9 considerably more durable than the Ka-Bar. Of course the M9 is not ideal as a bayonet due to the width of its blade. Fighters shouldn't be tempted to add it to the muzzle of a rifle except for parades or guarding prisoners.

The M9 MPBS has the "bells and whistles" common to the "fashion" of other military blades, including a wire-cutter cutout in the blade (which unfortunately makes it weaker) and a fine saw-toothed spine (which is, at least, less apt to catch in flesh or clothing than many larger-toothed designs, even though it has dubious cutting abilities). A lightening cut (sometimes mistakenly called a "blood groove") is located on the flip side of the blade opposite the sawteeth to keep the overall weight low.

The M9's sheath has some good features, including a container for a sharp-

The U.S. M9 bayonet has a blade similar to the Ka-Bar coupled with a modern plastic handle. The design promises to be popular with American troops.

ening stone and a second pouch that could hold odds and ends such as a small survival kit. The initial cost of the M9 was high due to competition with military sales, but it seems likely that the price will drop to a more reasonable level, making it ideal for those wanting a quality bowie-style bayonet. The M9 is available commercially from many suppliers, including the U.S. Cavalry store.

The U.S. Navy SEALs have adopted a knife based on the basic features of the M9. The SEAL knife has a shorter 5.33-inch blade and lacks the dubious wire-cutting abilities of its forebear while retaining the fine teeth of the M9.

Interestingly, the M9 replaces the M7 bayonet which, because of its narrow dagger blade, is actually efficient as a bayonet when mounted on a rifle. The M7 also makes an ideal dagger in its own right and, due to its low military-surplus price tag, is an excellent buy.

The M7 traces its lineage back to the M3 general-purpose knife created in 1943 and adopted by the U.S. Army. Light and well balanced, the M3 proved to be more effective than the heavy and awkward M1905 (for the Springfield rifle) and M1942 (for the Garand M1), both with 16-inch blades, as well as the M1, which was simply an M1942 with its blade ground to a shorter length.

The M3 has a 3.5-inch sharpened false edge running down its spine and a full edge down the front of its 6.75-inch blade. The cross guard is swept upward to accommodate the thumb as well as give a quick way to tell where the shorter false edge is in the dark. After its introduction, the M3 combat knife proved to be deadly effective and became popular among U.S. troops in the Pacific theater.

In 1944, when the M1 carbine was fielded, a new bayonet was needed since the firearm couldn't accept any of the bayonets designed for previous U.S. rifles. The popularity of the M3 knife caused designers to modify its basic layout with a new cross guard (with a muzzle ring) and a pommel with two spring-loaded latches to create the M4 Bayonet-Knife.

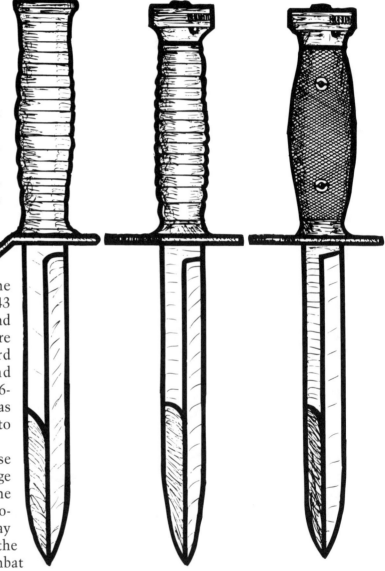

The U.S. M3 combat knife design (left) was the model for the M4 bayonet for the M1 carbine (center). A checkered plastic handle replaced the leather grip, making it more durable. This checkered handle/blade design was later adopted for use with the M16 rifle (right).

Though the new pommel marred the feel of the bayonet when compared to the original combat knife it was modeled after, it was nevertheless popular and effective.

With continued use in the Pacific, it was found that the leather handles (composed of washers mounted over the tang and held in place by the pommel) on the M4 were subject to rot. Molded rubber grips and wooden grips

Modern Combat Blades: The Best in Edged Weaponry

with plastic spacers at either end were created to solve the problem. Neither of these grip materials proved much more effective and were therefore replaced in 1956 by checkered plastic grips held in place by two cross screws.

The effectiveness of the M4 dictated the creation of the M5 bayonet for the Garand M1 rifle in 1955, replacing the M1942. The design was nearly identical to the M4 except for the modified attachment assembly to accommodate it to the Garand rifle. In 1957 the design was modified again to create the M6 bayonet for the new M14 rifle. Unfortunately, both the M5 and M6 bayonets are awkward to hold due to the shape of their grips and position of their release buttons, which lie on the forward end of the grip under the first finger when the bayonets are used as knives.

The M4 design was again called on for the M16 rifle. This new bayonet design was nearly identical to the M4 except for a larger hole in its cross guard to accommodate the greater diameter of the flash hider on the new rifle. The original experimental bayonets created by Colt (and issued to some air force units) had circular grooves on their plastic grips, making them appear similar to the original leather-gripped M4. The design finally adopted by the military as the M7 bayonet had plastic checkered grips identical to the late model M4's, thus avoiding much of the awkwardness of the M5 and M6 designs.

The standard M7 has a 6.5-inch blade. For those wanting the same style of blade in a longer length, Eickhorn created the SI-10A with a 9-inch blade. In a departure from the M3 design, the company sharpens the entire length of both sides of the blade rather than leaving a false edge on the spine. (Eickhorn also offers the standard-length blade with a wire cutter, which creates a fragile blade that is probably best avoided by most users.)

One quality fighting knife was created by Eickhorn through the expedient of replacing the ring and the pommel of the M7 bayonet with a standard knife grip and cross guard. This has created a near duplicate of the M3 that is

marketed as such by the company, even though the cross guard now lacks the upward-swept section on the thumb side of the blade. (As with most of the other bayonets and combat knives in this chapter, the Eickhorn variants of the M7 design are offered by Sherwood International.)

Prior to World War II, British Captains William E. Fairbairn and Eric A. Sykes, two soldiers with much firsthand knowledge of combat, created their Sykes-Fairbairn Commando knife with an eye toward making a weapon that was designed specifically for killing an enemy quickly and efficiently. Their design is still used by the SAS and is often seen in the hands of elite troops. It is variously known as the Sykes-Fairbairn, S-F (or F-S), or Commando knife.

As mentioned in the previous chapter, wartime demands forced manufacturing shortcuts. Some of the issue S-F knives were overtempered and had a tendency to break at the thin point and the grip/cross guard. Nevertheless, the S-F proved to be an effective weapon and was well-liked by the troops using it. With its round metal grip and narrow, 7-inch blade, it was designed solely for thrusting attacks and is both comfortable to hold and lightweight, making it first choice of many "pros." (For a detailed look at the development and variations of the S-F knife, see Leroy Thompson's *Commando Dagger*, available from Paladin Press.)

Several manufacturers make cheap reproductions of the S-F available for as little as $10, but buying one of these makes little sense because quality Commando knives made by Sheffield in England can be purchased for less than $40 (from Atlanta

The Sykes-Fairbairn Commando knife, created by British Captains William E. Fairbairn and Eric A. Sykes.

Cutlery, among others). Those purchasing the "real thing" should also avoid the Sheffield "authentic" SAS Commando Knife with a gold-plated insignia on the handle; while pretty, the insignia gets in the way of the hand, making it more of a wall hanger than fighting knife.

U.S. military designers quickly adapted the S-F to their own needs. The V-42 Stiletto created for American and Canadian elite units (including the "Devil's Brigade") during World War II is nearly identical to the Commando in size and layout, with a 7.25-inch tapered blade having double edges, a round grip (the tang covered by leather washers in this case), and a "skull crusher" pommel of dubious use that ends in a sharp point. These knives are still available from several sources, including U.S. Cavalry, which sells an English-made version for around $190, making it less than ideal for anyone other than collectors.

The U.S. Marine Corp's Carson's Raiders adopted the U.S. Marine Raider Stiletto in 1942. Though the marines take credit for its design, a quick inspection shows it is nearly identical to the British Commando except for a larger cross guard and nongrooved grip. Like the V-42, the Marine Raider Stiletto is a collector's knife and commands a hefty price even for reproductions, making it unsuitable for those needing a serviceable combat blade.

A modern rendition of the V-42 has been created by knife maker Gil Hibben and marketed as the Silver Shadow. With a stainless steel 7.5-inch dagger blade and twisted wire-wrap handle, this knife is more durable than the prone-to-rust-and-rot design of the V-42 and Marine Raider Stiletto. Best of all, the 13-ounce knife costs *less* than reproductions of the other two knives due to mass production. The overall design is marred by a sharp "skull crusher" pommel, but those concerned with this can quickly round the point off with a file to make it an ideal combat blade.

Being more interested in saving the lives of Allied soldiers than glory, Fairbairn worked to create a new knife that would overcome the problems the S-F was experiencing in combat. In 1943, he used this information and, with the help of Col. Rex Applegate, created an improved design which had a wider, stronger

blade (more suited to slashing as well as stabbing attacks), a stronger tang to prevent breakage, and a flat grip that both gave better purchase when the user's hands were damp or bloodied and allowed the user to determine the orientation of the blade by feel.

Unfortunately, this new design came too late to be utilized by troops during World War II. The project was shelved and all but forgotten until 1980 when Applegate signed contracts with manufacturers to put the Applegate-Fairbairn knife into production. Today, many consider this the best combat knife available.

The U.S. private sector saw a number of excellent knife

The Applegate-Fairbairn combat knife was created for Allied troops but failed to be produced before the end of World War II.

designs during World War II as well. John Ek first started making combat knives for U.S. servicemen during the war. Though he died in 1976, his company continues to produce superb dagger-style combat blades similar to those first offered by the company's founder. Most of these daggers have 6.5-inch blades and, though similar in concept to the SAS or Commando knife, the Ek knives have wide, flat tangs that are extensions of the blade. These are covered by wood, plastic, or nylon cord grips, making them very strong.

Coupled with a wide blade that can be honed to razor sharpness (with a double edge or

Modern Combat Blades: The Best in Edged Weaponry

a single edge with a sharpened false edge), the Ek design doesn't suffer from the frailty of the S-F Commando knife and is also considerably easier to manufacture. Though most of the Ek combat knives lack a cross guard (instead having small serrations on the edge of the blade so the thumb can find purchase and the user orient the blade by feel), a few newer models are now offered with one.

W.D. "Bo" Randall was another knife maker who created knives for military personnel wanting to purchase their own blades due to dissatisfaction with weapons issued to them during the Second World War. The Randall Model No. 1 remains just as popular today as when it was first introduced. Its basic design has been refined, but it is still pretty much the same as the original knife, having a blade of 7 to 8 inches, a modified bowie shape, and a sharpened false edge. Unlike many other military knives, the Randall No. 1 has a pronounced ricasso (the squared-off, unsharpened section between the cross guard and the edge of the blade); this allows for greater control of the blade during camp chores by placing the first finger ahead of the cross guard. Most of these custom knives have full-length tangs threaded to accommo-

John Ek first started making combat knives for U.S. servicemen during World War II, and these superb dagger-style combat blades have been carried by American troops during all the country's conflicts since then.

date the attachment of the grip and pommel. The knives proved popular with military personnel during World War II, the Korean War, and later in Vietnam, and they continue to be in high demand by those wanting a combat blade. In fact, one of the early American astronauts, Gordon Cooper, even carried a Randall knife with him in his survival kit, making it one of the first knives to orbit the Earth.

The company is presently run by Bo's son, Gary Randall, and some twenty-four different models are offered by the knife craftsmen working there. Prices and workmanship border on those of custom knives. Randall's company offers a variety of styles, most having blades in the 7-inch range with a modified bowie style. The Randall Model No. 2 is a notable exception with its dagger design.

The popularity of Randall knives during the Vietnam War led to some rather odd copies. These apparently were created for MACV-SOG (Military Assistance Command Vietnam Studies and Observation Group), which conducted covert missions in Vietnam and surrounding countries. Since the operations needed "sterile" weapons that couldn't be traced directly to U.S. troops, the soldiers were given knives modeled after Randall's No. 1 but produced by Oriental (possibly Japanese) manufacturers without any distinguishing marks on the blade. These knives generally had blued blades and leather washer grips. Many believe that CIA had similar knives made for them as well, this time copying the Randall Model No. 3 with a longer clip point than the MACV-SOG model had.

Interestingly, the SOG knife has come full circle and is now copied by a new company in the United States: SOG Specialty Knives. (More information on the SOG copies of the MACV-SOG design, as well as spin-offs of the basic design, will be covered in Chapter 4.)

As with World War II, the Vietnam War spurred brand new knife designs aimed at servicemen dissatisfied with issue knives. One of the most popular newcomers is the Gerber Mark II dagger. Its cast aluminum handle and stainless steel blade make it nearly impervious to the elements. The knife's basic design was created by Captain Bud Holzman, modified by

Gerber, and tested and then remodified by the U.S. military. The results were marketed in 1966, and the blade quickly became a favorite of American troops stationed in or headed for Vietnam.

In 1970, serrations were added to either side of the flattened, double-edged blade of the Mark II, and these have remained ever since. Unlike teeth, the serrations actually do work well and cut some materials faster than can the sharpened edges of the 6.5-inch blade. In 1978, Gerber made further improvements to the basic design, adding a black finish to the comfortably contoured grip (the original knife had a gray finish); the "cat tongue" surface on these new grips aids in retention of the knife as well.

Currently, there are several models of the Mark II. The Wasp has plain double blades without serrations and a gray and black handle, the standard Mark II has a black handle and serrated edges, and the Mark II Midnight Stalker has its blade blackened. (There is a Mark I, a boot knife with a similar design but a shortened grip and a 5-inch blade.)

Unfortunately, the popularity of the Mark II has resulted in a huge number of copies, many cheap and poorly made, flooding the market. Given the comparatively low retail price of under $70 for a *genuine* Gerber Mark II, those wanting this knife should buy the real thing.

As might be expected, the U.S. military's M3 has influenced the design of several foreign bayonets and combat knives. The German G3 bayonet has a 6.5-inch blade nearly identical to the M3. The grip departs radically from the original design with an "elongated pineapple" look that many actually find more comfortable to hold than the M3's original grip. (Eickhorn offers a longer version of this with a 10-inch blade, the SI-14.)

Manufacturing considerations can also influence knife designs. Although the original Soviet SKS bayonet was a spike (which continues to be used by the Chinese on their more modern rifles), the USSR soon switched to a double-bladed folding bayonet similar to that utilized on World War II-vintage rifles but with a 7.87-inch blade. The replacement rifle for the SKS, the AK-47, was first fielded without a bayonet, but

The first bayonet created for the AK-47 had a double-edged spear point that proved to be expensive to produce and a poor camp knife as well.

the Soviet military soon decided to add one. The double-blade design of the SKS was adapted to the firearm but this time had a detachable assembly so the blade could be removed and used as a knife if needed.

In order to streamline manufacturing of the bayonets that the military wanted for its rifles, a simplified blade assembly mounted on an AK-47-style handle was introduced in 1968 for

The SVD bayonet was modified for use on the Soviet AK-47, AKM, and AK-74 rifles. This design influenced the design of the bayonet created for Eugene Stoner's rifles.

the SVD sniping rifle. This has a 5.19-inch flat-steel blade, edged on one side with a shallow saw back and wire-cutter hole that can be utilized with the scabbard to cut lightweight wire. Although the saw back and wire-cutting abilities of the bayonet are of dubious use, the edge of the blade can be honed to razor sharpness. Coupled with the fact that it could be manufactured inexpensively, it undoubtedly was popular with both troops and procurement officers alike.

Soon the SVD bayonet was modified for use on the Soviet AK-47, AKM, and new AK-74 rifles. The blade design would be ineffective on a rifle since the blade is too wide, but this is a moot point, especially given the greater utility of a single-edged blade. SARCO sometimes has Hungarian-made AK-47 bayonets that are nearly identical to the Soviet models and cost in the neighborhood of $23.

In the West, inventive genius Eugene

Stoner (who had developed the M16 rifle as well as the AR-18 and other military rifles), working in conjunction with A. Eickhorn, created a bayonet for his Stoner family of modular rifles. The Stoner Bayonet was, in fact, nearly identical to the Soviet SVD design, complete with wire-cutter scabbard and saw-toothed spine. The sawteeth are less obnoxious than most since they are shallow and therefore present less chance of snagging in flesh or cloth-

Eickhorn/Stoner-style bayonet with sheath. This bayonet has had its cross guard reversed for ease in using it as a knife. Note the user-modified grip that has been rounded to help in retention of the bayonet.

ing. Nevertheless, the capability to cut thin wire or saw through wood is of dubious use since both tasks are accomplished more efficiently with a few sharp blows from the sharpened blade.

Although the Stoner rifle never became popular due to the success of the M16, the bayonets continue to be offered by Eickhorn since they fit on the M16 rifle as well as the many other military rifles that accept the M16 bayonet. Currently, Eickhorn offers seven different versions of these. Three are bayonets with 7-inch blades, one having a bottle opener hook built into the cross guard along with wire cutter, one without the bottle opener but with the wire cutter, and one that is simply a bayonet. The 10-inch version is offered only with the wire-cutting capability. By substituting the ring mount and attachment pommel with plastic moldings, the

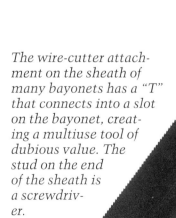

The wire-cutter attachment on the sheath of many bayonets has a "T" that connects into a slot on the bayonet, creating a multiuse tool of dubious value. The stud on the end of the sheath is a screwdriver.

Eickhorn has created an excellent combat knife by simply placing a standard grip on its 10-inch Stoner bayonet.

company has created two combat knives with 7-inch blades (with and without wire-cutting capabilities) and one 10-inch version (with a wire cutter).

The plastic grips on all of these Stoner knives and bayonets have a ribbed, squared-off design that isn't very comfortable to hold. Users will find that rounding the grips off with a wood rasp can greatly improve the handling characteristics of these knives.

Another variant of the USSR/Stoner design is the U.S. Navy's combat knife, the Mark 3, Modification 0. This has a 6-inch blade with sawback-style serrations along one side of the spine. With its excellent M7-style grip, this is a very comfortable knife with a strong blade capable of taking a sharp edge.

Another excellent combat knife manufactured by Eickhorn is the Austrian Army combat knife with a 6.5-inch blade (complete with a bottle opener in the cross guard). Glock, which manufactures the pistols adopted by the Austrian military, has also won contracts to manufacture these knives. The Austrian knife design is excellent for slash-style combat, and the blade is narrow enough to be capable of successful jabs as well. The blade also takes a sharp edge thanks to its hollow grind. Unfortunately, many of these are being made with saw-toothed backs—a temptation that manufacturers and military procurement committees just don't seem to be able to resist. The Eickhorn version of this knife is available from

Sherwood International, while Gutmann offers the Glock version in the United States.

The Bundeswehr's German Army combat knife, manufactured by Puma-Werk Lauterjung & Sohn as well as Eickhorn, has a 5.625-inch blade and plastic handle. The blade is thick enough for heavy utility use, and the plastic handle and cross guard help keep the knife's weight down to 6.5 ounces. It is available in the United States from Sherwood International.

The Spanish Army knife, the *Cuchillo de Monte*, or "knife of the mountains," is another popular blade that's being imported into the United States. This knife has a "big belly"

The Bundeswehr German Army knife, imported to the United States by Sherwood International, is a strong but lightweight fighting blade.

blade with a wide curve to its forward edge, similar to that of a surgeon's scalpel, giving it excellent cutting abilities (though to the detriment of its penetration capabilities for jabbing attacks). The black polyimide grip is an excellent design that most users find very comfortable; checkering and a swelled pommel aid retention even when the hands are wet. About the only drawback to the knife's design is a double row of sawteeth down its spine. The blade measures 7.125 inches, and the knife generally comes with an issue sheath made of ABS plastic and canvas.

A similar Spanish-made knife, the Para-military Knife, is manufactured by Eladio Muela and imported into the United States by Atlanta Cutlery. This knife couples the excellent grip of the Spanish military knife with a more conventional blade capable of both slash and thrust-style attacks. Additionally, it has replaced the sawteeth of the original with effective scallops.

The Chinese Armed Police knife has a unique design—the blade retracts into the handle so only the tip is covered by the scabbard. When the knife is drawn by pressing a release button, the scabbard retains the blade long enough for the 5.375-inch dagger blade to be telescoped out of the handle and locked in its extended position. The handle of the knife is plastic and the workmanship generally crude. With extended use, the blades often develop a lot of play in their open position. The

The Spanish Army Cuchillo de Monte is another popular blade that's currently being imported into the United States. It makes an excellent combat knife.

Armed Police knife makes an interesting collector's piece, but it is not ideal for combat use.

• • • • •

Unlike commercial knives, military combat knives and bayonets tend to be understated in design. Whether of a more utilitarian bowie configuration or the deadly efficient dagger design, these are businesslike weapons that carry relatively low price tags, making them sound buys for those wanting the best in compact weapons for a minimal amount of cash.

Chapter 3

POCKETKNIVES, BUTTERFLIES, AND SWITCHBLADES

olding knives have always had an important advantage over fixed-blade knives—they are easy to carry and easy to conceal. While few civilians would openly wear an M3 combat knife on their belt, most wouldn't think twice about carrying a folding knife in their pocket, in a pouch on their belt, or (in the case of the fairer sex) in a purse. Likewise, a law enforcement officer seeing a sheathed knife is apt to have a chat with the owner and possibly take him in, depending on how restrictive the laws are in the area. The same policeman wouldn't think twice about seeing a pocketknife on a belt, in a purse, or bulging in a pocket. So folders have an air of respectability that can be useful to those wishing to be armed without attracting undue attention from the law enforcement establishment or other citizens.

(Oddly enough, some folders actually break local laws passed during the 1950s when legislators decided they could break up teenaged gangs with restrictive laws. The gangs are still there but are now armed with firearms. Consequently, these laws are often ignored by officers *provided* they aren't out to run the owner of the knife in. A wise citizen will be aware of the local and state laws in his area and avoid doing anything that might cause him to be searched or harassed.)

Since folders can be carried easily, they are more likely to be used by civilians for self-defense than the combat knives and bayonets mentioned in the previous chapter; a folder in the hand is worth twelve bayonets tucked away in a storage cabinet. Consequently, while folders aren't normally a first choice as combat knives, they are more common in actual fights among civilians than their more deadly military counterparts.

Of course not just any folder will work. Folders with blades that don't lock open are ruled out since having a blade clamp shut on the fingers during combat isn't conducive to victory. Likewise, folders with short blades will often be unsuitable, though with some it is possible to shift the hand to a lower hold on the grip, in effect extending the reach of the blade. If the knife's liner and scale grips are thin enough, the grip will follow the blade into a wound, making it capable of reaching the depths of a longer blade.

Ideally, blades on a combat folder should be at least 4 inches long or, if local laws make this length impractical, then as close to 4 inches as possible. Preferably, the blade should be 6 inches or more, but this isn't practical with a folder that must be carried on the person without attracting attention.

A suitable combat folder will have a grip that affords the hand a tight purchase so the knife isn't lost if the fingers become wet or bloody. The design of the grip should keep the hand from sliding forward toward the blade during a thrust; knives that have slick handles can have their grips and liners grooved or checkered to make them more secure. Slick metal, pearl, or plastic grips are less than ideal, while grooved, rubberized, or checkered plastic grips may be suitable.

Finger swells and cross guards may also help, *provided* they don't interfere with the fighter's chosen hold. Many grips with grooves are not the right size for larger or smaller hands, and most are designed for a hammer grip, making the fencing grips nearly impossible.

The locking mechanism of the blade must keep it in place even if tremendous pressure is placed on the blade. This means the release must be recessed or otherwise placed so it can't be released inadvertently by any of the fingers even when grappling with an enemy or when the blade is shoved toward its closed position. Generally, heavy steel spring locks running down the spine of the grip will hold up better to such abuse than will split-liner locks that hold the blade in place with only a thin piece of spring metal—usually brass—inside the grip. When excessive pressure is applied to a liner lock, it often fails. (The only exceptions to this are titanium liner locks, but these are found only on expensive custom folders.)

Spine-spring locking mechanisms that don't lock securely in a deep notch in the blade aren't any better. Buyers should examine the locking mechanism carefully to be sure it is robust enough to keep a blade open at a critical moment. The cut in the back of the tang should be deep (this can be viewed through the front

opening in the grip liners when the blade is folded shut); if this cut is shallow, it can quickly fill with grime and the lock will fail.

Among the strongest locking mechanisms currently in use is what has become known as the "three-point system." It's used by most makers of quality folders, including Spyderco, SOG, Cold Steel, and AMK in its SERE series of knives. Even this locking mechanism will fail if enough pressure is placed on the spine of the blade, but it is the strongest system commonly available for folders until the four-point system (currently being played with by some knife makers) is perfected or someone develops a radical new system.

The rivets holding the lock spring and the lock itself (if they are separate parts rather than a single unit) should not come loose and release the blade. These rivets should be seen on either side of the grip. Steel rivets are preferable to brass. The spring action should be strong enough to keep from releasing the blade during jarring blows to the mechanism; while a weak spring will make the lock easy to use, it will also make it apt to come loose at a critical moment.

While quality folders will keep the blade locked in place during most violent contacts, they will fail if enough force is put on the blade from its spine. There is no way a folder with a half-inch tang will be capable of performance on a level equal to a full-tang, fixed-blade fighting knife. Users of folders must be aware of this fact and tailor their defensive attacks to avoid putting excessive pressure on the spine of the blade. Slashing is the safest form of attack, and jabs to soft parts of the body are possible provided a lifting action isn't used once the blade has entered the foe's body. Careful practice to hone fighting skills that won't break the folder's lock mechanism is essential.

Price doesn't always determine the strength or durability of a folder, but supercheap folders will often be just that: super cheap. The purchaser should check over his folder carefully and recheck it regularly to be sure it is in dependable condition.

By the same token, knives that are carried regularly will become dirty quickly. It is important to check pocketknives regularly, oil them, and clean out lint or other debris, being especially careful to check locking mechanisms.

It may seem like a minor consideration, but "what's in a name?" can be an important question to ask when buying a knife. The key here is for the purchaser to imagine standing in front of a jury trying to defend himself after wounding or killing a thug who was intent on doing bodily harm to the citizen. Having the prosecuting attorney point out that the name of the knife was the "Terminator," "Vigilante," or some such thing would certainly not help the defense lawyer. Care should be taken to pick a knife that will protect its owner in the courtroom as well as on the street if it ever comes to that.

Since most citizens will almost always be using their knives for self-defense, they won't have the luxury of slowly opening a folder (a luxury their attacker may, unfortunately, have). Which brings up another important specification for a combat folder: to be effective for defensive purposes, it must be capable of being opened rapidly.

As is often the case, politicians have made the job of self-defense even harder for those choosing a fold-

Switchblades are ideal for self-defense. The large button in the center of the grip releases the spring-loaded blade. The smaller button slides forward to lock the blade open or closed.

er. The U.S. Congress has passed restrictions on interstate sales of switchblades and gravity knives, and many state and local governments have outlawed these handy devices.

Switchblades are ideal for self-defense. The owner presses a button and the blade pivots open, often locking in place. Springers work much the same way, except the blade shoots straight out of the end of the grip rather than pivoting. The third type of knife generally restricted is the "gravity" or "inertia" knife, whose blade is dragged into place by gravity or inertia (generated by flicking the knife), where it usually is locked.

Many people think these knives are illegal to own, but in many areas this isn't the case. The problem for Congress is that these knives are arguably protected by the Second Amendment of the U.S. Constitution (which, with its ". . . right of the people to keep and bear arms shall not be infringed," gives citizens the right to own any type of arm which might be useful in military conflicts—not just firearms). Rather than break the Second Amendment of the Constitution (as is the case today with gun-control laws), in August 1958 Congress simply outlawed the *interstate sale* of these knives.

During the hysteria over street gangs during the late 1950s, many states also passed laws against these types of folding knives, and although this would appear to be violating the Second Amendment by depriving citizens of the civil right to own such knives, this apparently has never been challenged in court—partly because the law is seldom enforced. Interestingly, several groups are exempt from both the federal and most state laws. These include the police and military, since these knives are quite useful for many everyday chores as well as combat—oddly enough demonstrating, within the laws that outlaw these folders, that the devices are protected by the Second Amendment.

In addition to the groups exempted by the law declaring who can own quick-opening switchblades, gravity knives, and springers, there is a "loophole" in the federal law. Since only the sale or transportation of switchblades from one state to another is illegal, ownership and even sales *within* a state are legal as long as the knife remains within the state's borders and there are no local or state laws restricting its ownership. In fact, anyone making a switchblade, gravity knife, or springer, or altering a knife to these configurations can legally own one in many parts of the United States.

During the 1980s and into the 1990s, several companies took advantage of this loophole, selling unassembled kits through the mail to purchasers who could "manufacture" their own switchblade, usually by simply inserting a spring or attaching a few rivets to convert the

One of the last of the switchblade "kits" to be imported into the United States. Addition of a metal spring transformed the knife into a switchblade. Note the folding cross guard.

knife into a switchblade. Provided the "owner/manufacturer" didn't sell the switchblade to someone in another state or otherwise break the law, the knife was legal.

As is too often the case, the federal government stepped in, if not with legal grounds to stop the shipment, then with the simple expedient of denying importers the right to bring the easily converted knives into the United States. Soon the supply of foreign-made springer, gravity, and switchblade kits dried up—at least until American-made kits became available.

Custom-made switchblades as well as knives converted to this configuration continue to be legal in many areas and are therefore within the reach of do-it-yourselfers. Readers wanting a detailed look at the various switchblade mechanisms that might be adapted to such projects should read Ragnar Benson's excellent book, *Switch-*

blade: the Ace of Blades, available from Paladin Press.

Even in areas where gravity knives, springers, and switchblades have been outlawed, a person can still legally own a quick-to-open folding knife. As with many other restrictive laws, the laws against springers, gravity knives, and switchblades have become a challenge to inventors, who create knife-opening systems that circumvent the law. This is just what inventors have done with a nearly endless variety of legal opening systems, getting around nearly any and all federal, state, and local laws.

Under Congress's Public Law 85-623, which banned the interstate sale of switchblades, they are defined as knives which open automatically: 1) by hand pressure applied to a button or other device in the handle of the knife, or 2) by operation of inertia, gravity, or both. This leaves out several key mechanical possibilities, including buttons or other devices on the blade of a knife and possibly the combination of a button and gravity. Such possibilities are seen as challenges to creative minds.

One of the first of the commercially market-

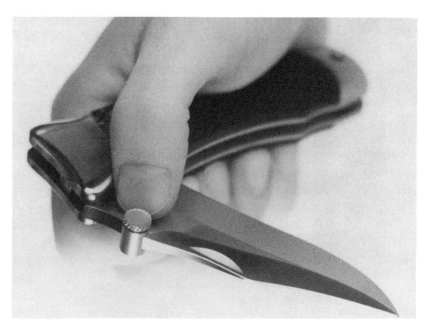

The One Arm Bandit allows a folder to be flipped open with the thumb. (Photo Courtesy of Y.B. Technology)

Modern Combat Blades: The Best in Edged Weaponry

ed inventions that created a legal quick-opening system was the Flicket, which consisted of a metal strip that could be fastened to the blade of almost any locking folder to create a small nub. This allowed the thumb to push and rotate the blade open in one quick motion. With a little practice, a person could open a folder just as quickly as he could a switchblade. The Flicket wasn't perfect, however, and it had a way of coming off. The company producing the device soon went out of business—but not before inspiring others to try similar techniques, the most common being the attachment of a peg or button to the blade of a custom-made folder to accomplish the same effect.

Perhaps the best of the inexpensive methods of converting a folder to a quick opener is the One Arm Bandit, first marketed by Y.B. Technology in 1990. This gadget fastens to the blade of any folder (with different versions available to accommodate varying blade thicknesses). Held in place with a set screw, the device creates a knob that is easily shoved by the thumb to open the blade rapidly.

The One Arm Bandit makes it possible for a purchaser to convert his favorite locking folder into a quick-to-open knife for the $10 cost of the kit. This means otherwise excellent knives like the Buck and Camillus folders—including multibladed utility knives like the Expedition series and the Tanto-bladed 894B—and custom or high-end production knives like the Al Mar SERE folders, can be "upgraded" to one-hand

openers. All that's needed for transformation to a splendid combat folding knife is the addition of a One Arm Bandit.

The Camillus Expedition folder is an excellent utility knife. The addition of a One Arm Bandit can make one of these blades quick to bring into action. Unlike many other multiblade designs, all three of these lock into place.

A few companies have created a similar thumb stud on their own knives by simply drilling a hole in the blade and then screwing a tiny knob into the hole (which allows left-handed customers to unscrew and reverse the stub). Among the best of these designs are three different models offered by SOG Specialty Knives: the SOG Winder I (with 2.625-inch blade), SOG Winder II (with 3.5-inch blade), and the Air SOG (with lightweight, 2.2 ounce, all-plastic body and 3.25-inch blade).

All three SOG knives have razor-sharp bowie-style blades and come with handy black nylon sheaths that can be mounted horizontally or vertically on a belt or suspenders as well as pinned inside clothing or a purse, making them extremely flexible to carry. The exteriors of these knives are checkered with a "rubbery" feel; retention is very positive, keeping the knife secure even during powerful jabs or if the hands are wet. Because the locks on these knives are located about midway on the spine of the grip,

A lightweight Buck folder can be transformed into a quick-open knife with the addition of a One Arm Bandit.

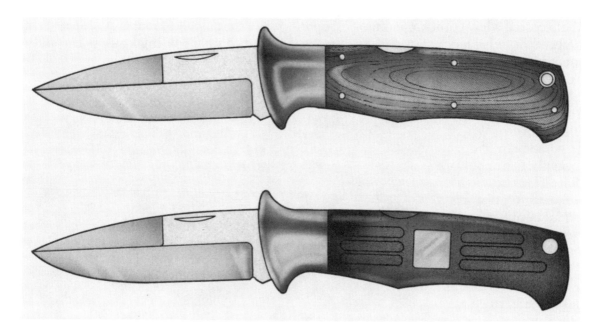

Two versions of Al Mar's SERE knives, which make excellent combat knives, especially with the addition of a One Arm Bandit. (Drawing courtesy of Al Mar)

it's possible to close them with one hand after a little practice, releasing the lock with the forefinger while "whipping" the blade shut against the side of the hip.

Perhaps believing that less is better, Spyderco has created the same effect by cutting a round hole in an extra-wide blade of a folder. This permits the thumb to engage the edges of the perforation to shove it open with a rapid flick. The blade can also be opened by grasping the cutout between the thumb and forefinger and whipping the grip of the knife to open it. This, however, leaves the blade between the fingers, so the knife has to be slid forward with a second movement, making it slower than opening the blade with the thumb.

Spyderco also has created a clip on the back of its Clipit line of knives which makes it possible to attach the knife to a pocket, inside a belt, or in any of a number of spots so it will "be there" when it's needed. This feature also

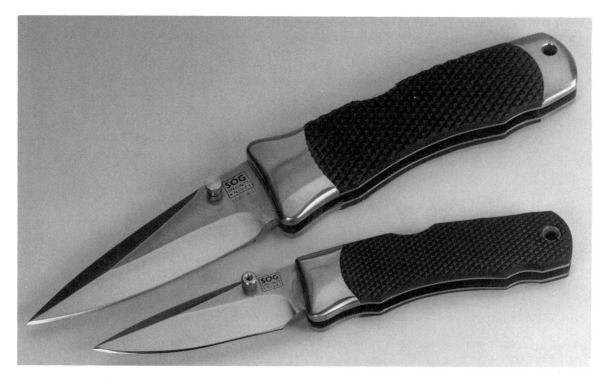

SOG Winder I (bottom) and SOG Winder II (top). (Photo courtesy of SOG Specialty Knives)

Modern Combat Blades: The Best in Edged Weaponry

speeds up the time it takes to bring the knife into play since it is unnecessary to open and extract the knife from a pouch or fight to get it out of a pocket.

The human engineering of the Spyderco knives is superb; the handles curve to accommodate the natural curve of the hand and point the blade forward for a nearly instinctive defensive stance. Because the locks on these knives are located about midway on the spine of the grip, it's possible to close them with one hand after a little practice. While this capability is not essential, it can often be helpful and might even save a user's bacon should he need to "melt into the crowd" after repelling an attack.

The blades are also superior, with an excellent serrated edge available as well as standard blades. The serrated edge is such a good cutter that the Clipits make excellent utility blades; this often guarantees that they'll be there when needed since the owner of the knife is used to carrying it around and operating it on a day-to-day basis.

In addition to its "custom" series of more expensive models, Spyderco has two production series of knives; one utilizes a stainless steel grip and blade while the other is comprised of a stainless steel blade and springs coupled with a lightweight Zytel body to create a superlightweight folder. The Police Model is first choice of the metal-gripped series of Clipits, with its sharp, 3.875-inch pointed blade capable of both thrusting and slashing defenses (and the name of this knife is in keeping with a "good guy" image).

Currently there are two models of plastic-gripped Clipits: the Delica with a 2.5-inch blade and the Endura with 3.5-inch blade. Of the two, the Endura is a better choice simply because it is longer; though this blade is a tad short for a true fighter, it's possible to grip it back to extend its reach. Fortunately, this is easy to do with the

Spyderco's excellent plastic-gripped Clipits make excellent defensive as well as lightweight utility knives. Shown here are the Endura (top) and the shorter Delica (bottom). (Photo courtesy of Spyderco)

Spyderco offers a wide range of quick-open locking folders. Here is the Police Model. (Photo courtesy of Spyderco)

well designed grips on the knives.

Al Mar Knives offers several series of folders with push buttons similar to SOGs. Some have blades too short for consideration as combat folders, but others have longer blades. Among these are the Quicksilver 2001 (with a straight-edge 3.375-inch blade; cost $36) and 2002 (3.375-inch serrated blade; $36), Stealth Hawk 1003SR (3-inch blade with a false edge and

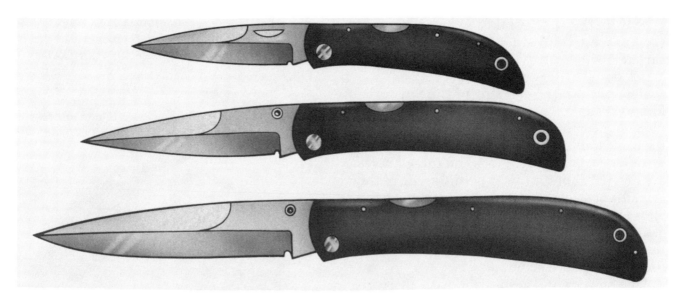

Three of Al Mar's excellent folders, the Hawk (top), Falcon (center), and Eagle (bottom). (Drawing courtesy of Al Mar)

Al Mar's excellent Quicksilver 2001 (top) and Quicksilver 2002 (bottom). (Drawing courtesy of Al Mar)

checkered rubber grips; $46), Falcon (3-inch blade with sharpened false edge; $77), and Eagle (4-inch blade with sharpened false edge; $89). The Al Mar knives have always been noted for quality and these are no exception; costs will vary according to options the customer chooses in the way of grips, carrying pouches, and so on.

Another one-hand opener of much different style is the balisong, or "butterfly knife," that traces its lineage back to the Philippines. The butterfly knife design potentially has one of the strongest lockups of all folders. Unfortunately, many cheap renditions are constructed of such poor materials that this potential isn't realized. But quality versions of this design, like those from Balisong, Pacific Cutlery, and Bench Made, are quite strong, and it is rumored that U.S. Navy SEAL teams often carry these knives.

Unfortunately, the butterfly knife demands some practice in order to flick it open easily, and the motion has to be executed with quite a flourish, making a covert opening—and surprise counterattack—hard, if not impossible. On the other hand, the opening of one of these can be so spectacular that a criminal may feel he's facing a seasoned fighter, thereby giving the owner a psychological edge—at least going into the fight.

As with the switchblade, Hollywood quickly latched onto this flashy knife, regularly placing it in the hands of criminals. Politicians, who often seem more influenced by the silver screen

Modern Combat Blades: The Best in Edged Weaponry

than by constituents, quickly designated these knives as the root of all evil, and in many cities, the butterfly knife is now illegal. In mid-1990, U.S. Customs announced that these knives could no longer be imported, so foreign-made versions are now collector's items.

Fortunately, enterprising U.S. manufacturers now create butterfly knives. The use of the knife in Hollywood movies died down, too, so many who were trying to stamp it out have set their targets on other issues. But the flashiness of this knife coupled with its bad-guy image makes it less than ideal for people looking for a self-defense blade, especially given the fact that other, easier-to-open knives are readily available.

As noted, the flashiness of the opening motion of a butterfly knife makes concealing the fact that it's being opened impossible. This creates another shortcoming for these knives since sometimes it's possible to anticipate trouble. Other folders that can be opened unobtrusively can be carried with an "ice pick" hold with the pommel toward the thumb and the blade extending downward. This permits nearly complete concealment of a knife in the hand with the blade alongside the arm, held beside the body. A casual observer will notice only that a person holding a knife in this manner has made a fist.

In fact, if confronted, the person can mount a wicked slash by

The Balisong, or "butterfly knife," from the Philippines. With practice, it is opened quickly.

bringing his hand upward, closing with his assailant, and then bringing the blade downward in an overhand stabbing action with the return stroke, faster than his foe can say, "This is a stickup." If the anticipated danger doesn't materialize, the folder can quietly be put away without further ado. This just isn't possible with a butterfly knife. Nonetheless, for those looking for a strong, swiftly opened folder who are willing to put in some time developing the skill to open it, the butterfly knife is worth considering.

The most common type of blade on the butterfly is single-edged, but drop-point bowies and Tanto-style blades are also seen. Handle materials vary considerably, with the best being stainless steel or aluminum with cutouts in the grips for added purchase.

"Gadgety" folders that can be opened with special lock releases or sliding buttons are also encountered. These often don't work consistently well, have weak locking mechanisms, or are hard to operate—especially in an emergency when the user's nerves and reflexes aren't in perfect order. Consequently, these usually are less desirable when compared to other knives listed above. (For those wanting to check into such knives, among the best are Parker Cutlery's SOK, the Gerber Bolt Action, and the antique Christy design available as a collector's knife.)

Though technically not a folder, a design that challenges the ban against switchblades, gravity knives, and springers from another direction is a sheath-type cover that's spring-loaded so it pops away to expose a blade. The first of these was the Tekna Micro-Knife (which has been discontinued); a newer example is the Black Magic (offered by U.S. Cavalry), which appears to be a NATO switchblade when open but actually uses the basic idea first demonstrated by Tekna with the added plus of a cover that can be replaced over the blade with a flick of a button (rather than manually, as is the case with the Tekna).

Neither of these knives is ideal since they're as long as a standard sheath knife, and the retractable cover is generally too flimsy to allow safe carry in a pants pocket. However, the basic idea could be modified so that the

Tekna Micro-Knife with sheath around blade.

Tekna Micro-Knife after button on top has been pushed, retracting the spring-loaded sheath to expose the blade.

sheath springs beyond the end of the blade, becoming the lower half of a grip for the user. This would create a more compact unit that would rival the switchblade in speed and ease of operation and would be nearly as secure as a fixed knife with no chance of the blade folding up into the grip when put under the stresses of combat.

It should be noted that cheap lockback folders with the release mechanism sticking from the spine of the grip can also be opened quickly with one hand by shoving down on the release with the first finger and flicking the blade so it flips open. (Because many of these knives are poorly finished, it is sometimes necessary to polish the base of the blade touching the lock mechanism before it will open easily.) With practice, this maneuver opens the blade so quickly that the knife is often mistaken for a switchblade by onlookers.

But most lockbacks with this design are cheaply made and won't stand up to heavy use, making them suitable only for slashing attacks; a thrust would likely cause the lock mechanism to fail. But they are inexpensive and some are very thin, making them easy to conceal even in the pocket of light summer clothing.

Among the best designs for such use is the inexpensive CAT knife, originally carried by German soldiers during World Wars I and II. Their design reduces the folder to its most basic components: a grip made of one stamped metal section coupled with a minimal lock and

spring. These knives were designed so the German military could produce them with little in the way of time, money, or materials—and from this standpoint, the CAT knife has to be viewed as a success.

In addition to the German-made version of this knife, Japanese copies are also imported into the United States. These are nearly identical to the original and also are inexpensive utilitarian folders.

Besides being capable of being opened with one hand, the CAT is only 1/4-inch thick and can be hidden in a pocket without the telltale bulge of most folders, an important plus. Japanese versions of the knife are available from Atlanta Cutlery, Gutmann, and others,

The inexpensive CAT knife design, originally carried by German soldiers during World Wars I and II. Shown here is a Japanese-made copy with its black paint finish worn off its grip.

with Gutmann also offering the German K55 model. Prices are generally under $17.

The dexterous can also (with lots of practice) snap many folders open by sliding their thumb against the side of the blade (one slip and they get cut doing this trick) or by grasping the blade between the thumb and forefinger and then flipping the body of the knife. The big problem with these techniques is the possibility of error when the heat is on and the adrenaline flowing (which makes the hands shaky and destroys concentration, among other things). Additionally, if the second method of flipping the knife open is used, the weapon must then be repositioned in the hand, actually making the opening slower than if both hands were used to simply open it in the first place.

With the addition of the One Arm Bandit,

Modern Combat Blades: The Best in Edged Weaponry

there are a number of excellent knives that would be suitable for self-defense. Among the best of these are the Al Mar SEREs (which stands for Survive, Escape, Resistance, Evasion), which were created in conjunction with the SERE operations within the Special Operations Command at Fort Bragg, North Carolina. (Al Mar was himself a Green Beret during the early years of U.S. involvement in Vietnam and has firsthand experience in what works in a combat knife.) The knives, the final result of this project, have stainless steel blades and scales on their grips designed to resist moisture damage. The blades have false edges that give them semidagger shapes and fine edges suitable for a wide variety of cutting chores.

The SERE Attack I series of folders have 3-inch blades, the Attack II, 3.5-inch, and the Attack III, 4.25-inch. Costs vary from around $100 to $200, depending on the type of grips, blade length, and so forth.

Camillus offers a number of "utility" lockbacks that would make excellent defensive knives with the addition of a One Arm Bandit. The Camillus double-bladed lockback Trapper or triple-bladed lockback Promaster series are good work knives for use in the field. Their specialty saw and knife blades lock in place, making them considerably safer than Swiss Army knives or similar folders that don't prevent blades from folding unexpectedly during cutting chores. While the double and triple blades make them a tad bulky, it may be better than carrying two knives, one for utility use and one for combat.

Some of the bulkiness of the knives can be eliminated by removing the Kryton scales and then carefully smoothing and reworking the grips, but this is a lot of work and normally not necessary. It also does away with the good grip surface these knives enjoy.

There are many lockbacks not listed in this chapter that might be suitable for some readers' combat needs, including "giant" lockbacks with 6-inch blades (some of these can actually be flipped open with a quick flick of the wrist due to the weight of the blade). But great care needs to be taken to examine any such knife for durability, strength, and suitable layout for use in combat. And those that can be flicked open through inertia weight of the blade are technically illegal, even if now sold openly.

As one might expect, the popularity of the Spyderco, SOG, and Al Mar knives has encouraged other manufacturers to create inferior imitations of their designs. As is often the case, you get what you pay for with these copies. Hopefully the imitators will also duplicate the quality of these blades in the near future.

It is also hoped that the "bird in the hand" utility folder won't go the way of the switchblade and its sister knives. But in the meantime, the wise U.S. citizen will purchase folders to suit his needs *before* more restrictive laws can be passed to outlaw yet another avenue of self-defense now open to him.

Chapter 4
THE MODERN BOWIE KNIFE AND ITS SPIN-OFFS

Combat blades have always captured the imagination. But not since King Arthur's legendary sword "Excalibur" (drawn from a stone and thrown back to the Lady of the Lake upon the king's death) has any blade seized the fancy of the public more than James Bowie's fighting knife. Though the original bowie knife is steeped in legend much like the weapon of the Arthurian hero of the Dark Ages, much is known about the more recent blade as well as Bowie himself.

Bowie was raised on a plantation in Louisiana in the early 1800s, where his father trained him and his brother Rezin Bowie, Jr., in the gentlemanly arts, including sword fighting, riding, and shooting. Additionally, the young men likely were nurtured with tales of combat since their father, Rezin Sr., had fought during the American Revolution with Francis "The Swamp Fox" Marion. Several ongoing feuds with neighboring families undoubtedly taught the boys lessons about combat, often firsthand.

Oddly enough, the first design of a unique bowie blade wasn't created by James Bowie but rather by his brother Rezin. According to the family history (recounted by their sister), Rezin Jr. was out hunting when he was attacked by a bull. When his single-shot rifle failed to stop the charging animal, the young Bowie attempted to dispatch it with his knife. In the confusion, his hand slipped past the grip and was so severely cut that his thumb was nearly severed.

Rezin escaped more serious injury, but he decided a better knife design than that of the hunting knife he carried was called for. Sitting down with Jesse Cliffe, the blacksmith who worked solely on the Bowie plantation, the two created a knife design that Cliffe fabricated from an old file and other odds and ends in his shop. The resulting knife is believed to have had a wide, long, single-edged blade with a round grip—sort of a heavy butcher knife with a fencing foil grip.

A short time later, Rezin Jr. gave the knife to his brother for self-defense after a member of a family that was feuding with the Bowies fired a shot at James, narrowly missing him.

The knife was soon to draw blood during what has since come to be known as the "Vidalia Sandbar" or "Sandbar Duel" (which, because it quickly escalated into a major fracas, more resembled a rumble between rival gangs than a gentlemen's duel). The combatants were deadly serious; during the fight, James was seriously wounded, but he managed to kill two of his foes and wound several others—using only his brother's knife.

Perhaps part of the bowie knife's popularity should be chalked up to good fortune and good press. The story of the knife fight spread as James recovered after chances of his survival were given as "slim to none" by the doctor attending him (according to the various accounts of the aftermath of the battle, at least). The story grew with each retelling. The first reports spread rapidly through New Orleans and from there by word of mouth across the West. Eventually, the narrative was being recounted in newspapers as far north as Chicago and New York. James had become a legend.

Legend overtakes fact regarding the origin of the knife James Bowie actually carried with him as he carved out a fortune in land and assets in Texas and Mexico over the next few years. One story holds that in 1830 he visited an extremely talented knife maker of the time, James Black, in Washington, Arkansas. Here, the story goes, Bowie showed the knifesmith a wooden model of the knife he had in mind. The knifesmith made the knife along with another having features he felt would make it even better.

Again, legends abound about the knife Black made (and there is even some doubt as to whether or not Black actually existed). Some said the blade was fashioned from a meteorite, giving it super strength; others claim that Black's secret knife-making processes—now lost—created a knife that never needed sharpening.

Another account claims that Rees Fitspatrick of Natchez, Mississippi, created Bowie's knife. This story is slightly more credible in that there are records of such a man having lived in the area, and he did make swords and knives.

The third theory of the origin of James Bowie's final knife is that it wasn't his invention at all, nor was it a new blade, but simply Rezin's original knife or a later one Rezin created and—as with the first—gave to his brother.

Which of these stories

No one knows what James Bowie's knife really looked like, but many authorities feel it may have looked something like this.

(if any) is correct will likely never be known. But lack of facts never stood in the way of legends, especially with a man like James Bowie.

On a return trip from Arkansas into Texas, Bowie had a chance to test his knife. According to his own account, he was attacked by three outlaws, apparently hired to kill him. According to Bowie, he decapitated his first assailant, disemboweled the second, and split the third one's head open from crown to shoulder. The public had another story to set tongues wagging.

(There has been speculation as to just how three men could be dispatched if they had ambushed a single man. It seems likely they were either outrageously poor tacticians when it came to staging an ambush, or there was more to the story than Bowie revealed. Nevertheless, it appears that Bowie's contemporaries believed him. This suggests that he must have been a skillful fighter—or storyteller—and that his assailants had poor reputations to start with.)

Bowie was to survive at least nineteen similar confrontations, suffer the loss of his wife and children in an epidemic, and eventually fight to the death at the Alamo. By the time of his death, he and his knife had achieved legendary status.

At the time the West was being settled,

firearms were marginal and unreliable, and backup weapons were needed. As stories of Bowie's exploits spread, men all across the West were asking for and buying "bowie knives"—often unaware of exactly what a bowie knife actually was other than big.

It is interesting to note that, even in the country's infancy, Americans tended to be "gadget oriented" and willing to believe that having the right tool would enable them to be like the person who had first succeeded with it. In fact, Bowie's knife wasn't nearly as important to his success in combat as was his skill in using it.

Unlike many conventional knife fighters of the time, Bowie apparently held his knife like a sword, thrusting and slashing rather than using an ice pick hold to make awkward, downward stabs. Additionally, it appears that he used the tactic of attacking his opponent's ability to wield the weapon, slashing the enemy's knife hand until the foe was unable to wield his weapon to its full potential. Then Bowie most likely moved in for the kill. If this is true, then Bowie should be credited with popularizing the American knife bearing his name as well as the modern style of fighting.

For the two decades following James Bowie's death at the Alamo in 1836, demand for bowie knives skyrocketed. American knife manufacturers couldn't meet the demand, and soon, knife and sword makers in Sheffield, England, and elsewhere were switching from making royal cutlery for the English government to creating bowie blades for the more lucrative American frontier.

As with many of the old standbys of the 1800s, technology finally caught up to and displaced the bowie blade. As the pistol and rifle became more reliable and the firepower of compact revolvers like the Colt became available (with lever-action rifles on the horizon), the need for a heavy backup weapon like a bowie diminished and finally all but disappeared. By the end of the Civil War, the demand for bowies had dried to a trickle. Only when hand-to-hand fighting returned in the trenches of Europe during World War I and the nocturnal commando raids of World War II, Korea, and Vietnam did the bowie blade again become

popular, though in the form of an anemic weapon with a blade only a fraction of the size likely sported by the original bowie knife.

In the mid-1800s, when books and even newspapers were not yet widespread and photography was in its infancy, most buyers of bowie knives had no idea what the real thing looked like. Consequently, "bowie knives" of the period often had dagger shapes with two sharpened edges, lacked cross guards, or came with features not commonly seen on what has come to be known as the bowie knife.

Yet one can hardly fault those buyers of yesteryear because, when the smoke and legends clear, today's scholars still have almost no clue of exactly what the original knife looked like. There are several likely candidates, but no one really knows for sure.

Nevertheless, the "bowie knife" has come to be accepted as having several key features (whether or not the original did): a thick, single-edged blade (often with a sharpened false edge along the first few inches of its spine and usually with a concave curving "clip" point), a cross guard to keep the fingers from slipping forward onto the blade, and a blade length of at least 9 inches (though this feature often is missing on modern knives having "bowie-style blades" of 7 inches or less).

Although many of today's "combat bowies" have blades with stunted lengths, more than a few manufacturers sell knives that James and Rezin Bowie would have recognized as being similar to their own. Many are still handmade with ornate handles and cross guards like the one James Bowie likely had, and some even have etched blades and exhibit graceful lines and exquisite workmanship.

In fact, for many craftsmen the bowie knife has become a work of art, far divorced from its original purpose of dispatching a raging bull or slitting the throat of an opponent before he could do the same to you. And while these "pretty" knives certainly can be pressed into service as combat weapons, the cost of such pieces of art makes them less likely candidates for such tasks.

Fortunately, the utilitarian bowie-pattern knife is still in demand, and production bowies carrying price tags under $200 are available to today's shopper. They make an ideal choice for anyone wanting a bladed weapon for self-defense rather than hanging on a den wall.

One company producing a variety of bowies is Gerber. Its Australian and Outback (American-style bowies made famous by the *Crocodile Dundee* movies) both sport 9.5-inch blades and slight clip points, wide cross guards, and "coffin" grips (i.e., symmetrical, flattened, with a three-sided end that makes the grip similar in shape to a nineteenth-century coffin). The Australian has a "white" stainless steel blade and the Outback has a blackened stainless steel blade. Each weighs 17.6 ounces and has an overall length of 14.75 inches. Cost is in the $100-$140 range, depending on the dealer.

Gerber's Predator and BMF have 9-inch stainless steel blades, and each weighs a tad over a pound. The BMF is cursed with a saw-toothed spine right out of Hollywood, making it less than ideal for combat. The Predator lacks a thumb guard but has a forward cross guard, which is not necessarily a drawback and may appeal to some buyers. Both blades have heavy pommels that

Gerber's Australian has a 9.5-inch blade and a "coffin" grip.

Gerber's Predator with a 9-inch blade and a "skull crusher" pommel.

aren't pointed, making them less apt to wound the wielder even if they will seldom be used. Cost is in the $160-$235 range.

Cold Steel offers the Trail Master Bowie with a 9.5-inch stainless steel blade, brass cross guard, and textured Kraton handle (a rubbery plastic that acts somewhat like a shock-absorber when the knife is in heavy use). The Trail Master's blade is made of Carbon V, which makes it slightly stronger and better able to hold an edge. On the downside, the blade is prone to rust and therefore demands special attention. Weight is 16.9 ounces, and the cost is from $180 to $225.

SOG Specialty Knives produces two excellent bowies: the Tigershark with a 9-inch "white" blade and the nearly identical Midnite Shark with a blackened blade. Both have aggressive false blades running back nearly to the cross guards; this makes them more capable than other bowies at jabbing cuts as well as the traditional slash a massive knife like this can deliver. These knives both utilize a high-carbon steel in their blades, which gives them added strength and the ability to hold an edge, but also requires extra care to prevent rust.

The 17.8-ounce SOG Tigershark and Midnite Shark both feature shock-absorbing Kraton

Modern Combat Blades: The Best in Edged Weaponry

Cold Steel's Trail Master Bowie with a 9.5-inch stainless steel blade, brass cross guard, and textured Kraton handle.

handles that have the cross guards molded into them. In addition to making the knives "quieter" (no noise is produced if the cross guards hit other equipment on the belt), these grips are also more comfortable than those of many other knives, especially when a heavy blow is delivered. The Tigershark costs $140 while the Midnite Tiger runs about $20 to $30 dollars more.

The HSEK (High Speed Edge Knife) made in Japan by master designer Hajime Nagai is imported into the United States by Spyderco. This knife has traditional bowie lines with a polished brass guard, but it features micarta grips for added durability. The 9.4375-inch blade has a short, sharpened false edge; the full edge has a "high-speed" edge with a clamshell profile that is said to improve blade penetration during a cutting stroke. Cost is $156.

Al Mar's Alaskan dwarfs most other bowie knives with its massive 12-inch blade and hefty 23.3-ounce weight. The blade is hollow-ground, helping it keep its edge, but it is carbon steel, so users must take precautions to avoid rust. The grip is wood and the cross guard stainless steel. Being of the quality of a custom-made knife, it also carries a higher price tag than most others in this group—from $225 to $250.

The SF-10 is a smaller (though still massive) bowie also offered by Al Mar that sports a 10-inch blade, rounded grip, and a file-style saw-toothed spine. The cord-wrapped grip is hollow, allowing for storage of a "survival kit" for those needing such a capability; a rubber gasket keeps the compartment water-proof.

Catoctin Cutlery carries the Blackjack brand of knives, including the Anaconda I and II Bowies. These have stainless steel blades and Kraton handles with brass cross guards. The Anaconda I has an 8-inch blade (technically making it an inch shy of bowie standards) while the Anaconda II has a 10.25-inch blade. Cost ranges from $48 to $99 for these knives.

Catoctin also offers a more traditional Blackjack Bowie designed by Bill Moran, the founder of the American Bladesmith Society. The design was originally created in 1967 when a knife was made for blade expert, writer, and editor Ken Warner, who was getting ready for a "trip" to Vietnam.

This knife is now being copied and offered commercially as the Warner/Moran Camp Bowie. It has a 10-inch carbon steel blade, double brass guard, and rosewood handle. Departing from the traditional bowie pattern somewhat, the blade has a "spear point" rather than a hooked clip point. Cost is $120 to $200.

And of course there are reproductions of the

SOG
Tigershark
in front of its
namesake.
(Photo cour-
tesy of SOG
Specialty
Knives)

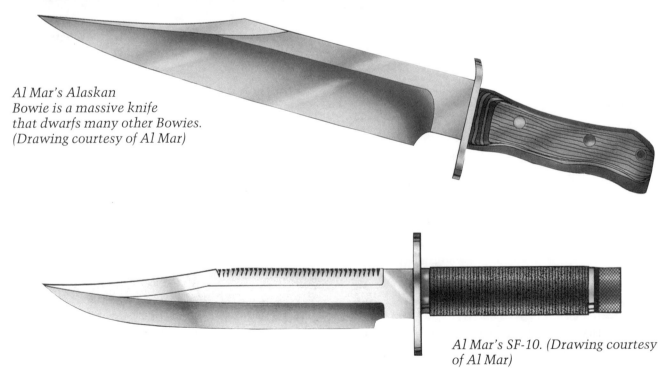

Al Mar's Alaskan
Bowie is a massive knife
that dwarfs many other Bowies.
(Drawing courtesy of Al Mar)

Al Mar's SF-10. (Drawing courtesy
of Al Mar)

Modern Combat Blades: The Best in Edged Weaponry

knives used in the first three (with possibly more to come) *Rambo* movies. The sawteeth on the back of all of these make them less than ideal as combat blades, so they are best dismissed or delegated to the cabinets of those who collect knives.

In addition to the quality knives offered by the manufacturers above, less expensive bowies are sold by several major companies. While inexpensive combat knives generally are a poor investment, especially given the fact that the purchaser's life may be on the line, the bowie knife is "overdesigned" in terms of strength. Where an inexpensive dagger or smaller combat blade might snap off when stressed beyond its capacity, it's hard to imagine a combat situation where enough stress is placed on even a cheap bowie to snap its blade. Consequently, those on a limited budget might want to consider acquiring one of these and then adopt the "slash and thrust" style best suited to the heavy bowie knife.

Among the bowies offered by Tiffin Family Knife Company is the Giant Hunting and Survival Knife (all bases covered with this name—product number HK6200 selling for $38). This knife has a beefy 3-pound weight and a 15-inch stainless steel blade. Other offerings include the simply titled Bowie (number BB1 for $12.50) with a 10-inch blade, and the oddly named Top Quality Antique Bowie (ABB2 with wood handle for $18, or ABB2-H with a buffalo-horn handle for $25).

If the requirement of a minimum blade length of 9 inches for a bowie is discarded, a wealth of "mini-bowies" can be found. Many of these are suitable for, or even designated as being for, combat. These vary from inexpensive (under $10) imported hunting knives from major suppliers like the Tiffin Family Knife Company to expensive custom-made blades. Production of mini-bowie knives by companies like Buck, Western, Schrade, Tekna, Puma, Gerber, Al Mar, Cold Steel, and many, many other manufacturers has created a bewildering variety of models. Throw in antique and custom knives and the choices for a buyer are nearly unlimited.

For those wanting a "special" short-bladed bowie-style knife to suit their needs, there's undoubtedly a hunting, survival, camping, or whatever bowie from one maker or another that's got *just* the features needed. The only obstacle is the time required in haunting the knife shows, reading the dealers' catalogs, and exploring antique and sporting stores to locate the perfect bowie.

One way of shortening the search is to first check what's available in the way of military blades. The best quality-per-dollar spent on these smaller combat bowies is found in the military knives and bayonets covered in Chapter 2. These are almost all well made and, except where noted, well designed, and mass production keeps prices down to reasonable levels.

Another area to search is companies that make production models aimed at military users. Randall and Al Mar are good places to look for short knives with bowie lines *if* price is no object. Randall's Model No. 12 knives, for example, have bowie-style blades. While the price of these is steep ($190 and up), they are well made and have long been the choice of those looking for the perfect combat blade. (The Model 12 is also offered with a 9- or 12-inch blade to create a traditional bowie, but the $320-plus price tags put these out of the reach of most buyers.)

A.G. Russell has a series of Combat Bowies with 7.5-inch blades and stag scale or Zytel (nylon with fiberglass reinforcement) handles. Cost runs from $80 to $230, depending on the type of handle chosen.

Several mass-producing manufacturers offer short-bladed bowies in the mid-price range designed specifically for combat. Ek, for example, has several Commando knives with bowie-style blades (rather than their more common dagger design). These have 6.75-inch blades coupled with "handprint" and cord-wound grips found on the company's other models. Cost runs around $125.

Blackjack's Mamba 7L ($60) has a 7-inch stainless steel blade and Kraton handle, and its Ozark Bowie ($60) has a 7-inch carbon steel blade with Kraton handle. The company's Smoke Jumper ($50) has a 5-inch carbon blade. All of these have modified bowie lines.

SOG offers several excellent small bowies. The Government (with stainless steel blade) and

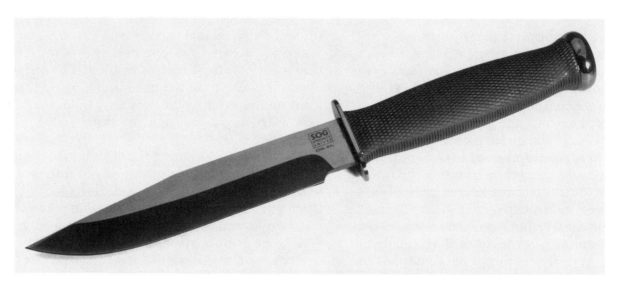

SOG Recon Government with razor-sharp blade and black finish. (Photo courtesy of SOG Specialty Knives)

SOG Tech I (bottom) and Tech II (top) have stainless steel blades and Kraton handles for a secure grip. (Photo courtesy of SOG Specialty Knives)

The SOG Bowie is a near duplicate of the Vietnam War blade carried by many American Special Forces troops on covert missions. (Photo courtesy of SOG Specialty Knives)

Modern Combat Blades: The Best in Edged Weaponry

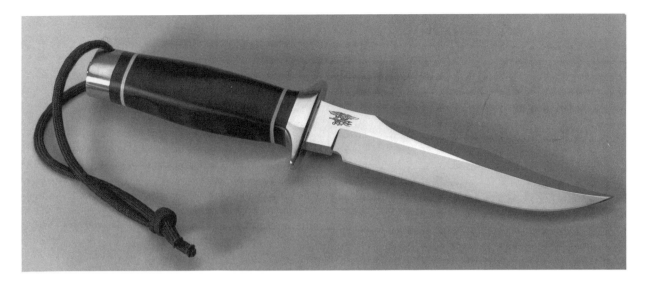

SOG's Trident couples the design of the Vietnam-vintage SOG Bowie with a stainless steel blade and a grip of micarta washers for a tough, moisture-proof knife. (Photo courtesy of SOG Specialty Knives)

Recon Government (with black-finished carbon blade) have 6.25-inch blades with heavy metal pommels, steel cross guards, and Kraton wraparound checkered grips. Cost is around $65.

Other excellent offerings from SOG are the Tech I (with 5.75-inch blade) and Tech II (7-inch blade). Both have stainless steel blades 1/4-inch thick with beveled-edge clip points, Kraton handles, and brass cross guards. Like other SOG knives, they are comfortable to hold and use, thanks to careful human engineering and choice of materials. Cost is under $100 for either of these fine blades.

SOG has also created several copies of the basic American Special Operations Group

knife of Vietnam War vintage. A near duplicate of the original knife, the SOG Bowie has a leather grip and a 6.25-inch blued blade.

The SOG Trident is nearly identical to the SOG Bowie but has a stainless steel blade and micarta washer grip, creating a knife ideal for use in or near the water. These excellent fighters cost $220.

The Gryphon M30A1 knife, designed by noted knifesmith Robert Terzuola, also displays bowie lines. The M30A1 has a 6.25-inch blade with a tough Zytel grip and cross guards molded around its tang. Cost is $225.

A number of the German-made Puma knives also have bowie lines. Most of these use

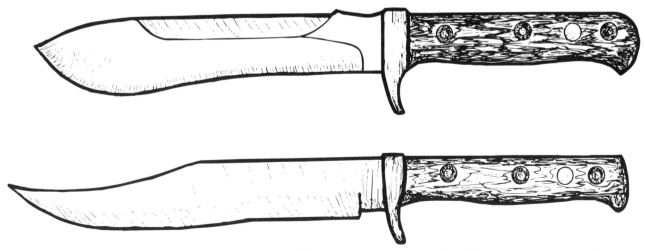

Puma offers a number of knives with bowie-style blades. Shown here are the White Hunter (top) and the Bowie (bottom).

The Modern Bowie Knife and Its Spin-Offs

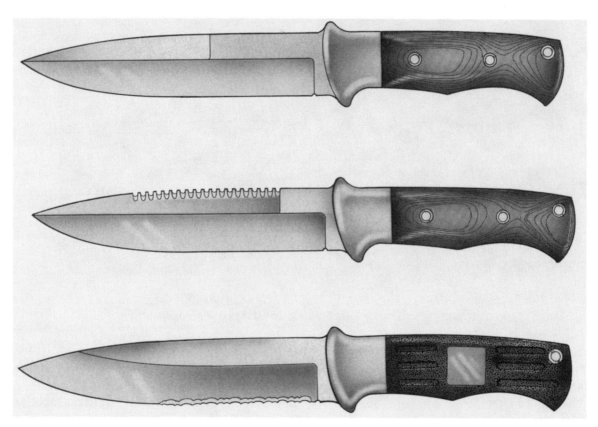

Three of Al Mar's SERE fixed-blade bowie-style knives. (Drawing courtesy of Al Mar)

traditional stag handles with a forward steel cross guard for the fingers but none for the thumb. These range in size from the Skinner, with 5-inch blade and 5.9-ounce weight, to the Bowie (6.5-inch blade, 7.3-ounce weight), White Hunter (6 inches, 9 ounces), Original Bowie (8 inches, 13.7 ounces), and Elite Hunter (8.5 inches, 21.6 ounces), with costs ranging from $180 to around $450.

Al Mar has created a series of small bowie-style knives that have come "in through the back door" since they are spin-offs of the SERE folders described in Chapter 3. Unlike the folders, these have fixed blades and therefore have smaller grips in relation to their cutting edges. They are available with 5- or 7-inch blades, with a choice of false edge or serrated spine with the 5-inch blades or serrated or standard one-edged blade with the 7-inch models. Cost varies from $196 to $220 according to grip scale materials and blade style and length.

Al Mar's Special Forces One-Zero, or SF/SOG. (Drawing courtesy of Al Mar)

Al Mar's Special Forces One-Zero, or SF/SOG, was designed with U.S. Special Forces in mind. The knife sports a 6.5-inch blade and has finger swells molded into the grip.

• • • • •

Whether a fighter picks a monster bowie

with a 12-inch blade, a custom knife with a $400 price tag, or a diminutive mass-produced "hunter" with a 6-inch blade, the bowie-style knife can serve him well. It has long been a favorite from the time James Bowie started the legends about this rugged combat blade. It has traveled to distant shores in the hands of American fighters since and doubtless will continue to do so well into the twenty-first century.

Chapter 5

DAGGERS AND STILETTOS

The ancient dagger-style weapon dates back at least to court intrigues in medieval Europe and the Middle East, and it might be argued that many Greek and Roman weapons displayed all the characteristics of large daggers with slender, double-edged forms and wicked points. Fighters from Julius Caesar (who instructed his soldiers to use the points of their short swords when a battle needed to be won in a hurry) to duelers of the seventeenth, eighteenth, and nineteenth centuries (when narrow-bladed swords replaced their wide-bladed ancestors) to modern-day tacticians like Sykes, Fairbairn, and Applegate have all concluded that a weapon capable of delivering a quick, lethal jab will end a fight with minimum chance of injury to the user of the blade.

From the first, daggers were recognized as being dangerous weapons to the powers that be. Easily concealed, the knives defy visual searches designed at disarming citizenry. Peasants in the Middle Ages discovered that narrow blades could even be used to kill a knight in armor by reaching between armor plates and stabbing through chain mail, making a good dagger more effective than a sword or battle ax once a fighter closed with his opponent.

Needless to say, the dagger and its cousin, the stiletto, have been outlawed by overbearing governments during various times in history almost from day one. The same is true today in the United States—virtually every blade in this chapter is illegal to carry concealed on one's person without a special permit in all fifty states. In most areas, however, these weapons can be used for home defense, making them of interest to many citizens.

For those searching for a modern combat blade, it's interesting to note that, when knives were actually being used for hand-to-hand combat on a regular basis, the narrow dagger blade almost always met with greater acceptance than wider or heavier designs. Swords "evolved" into the short Roman sword; in Europe during the Middle Ages, the trend went from heavy broadswords to thin, narrow-bladed versions (with the only "throwback" being the saber, which was required more for length of reach and speeding horseback charges than as a utilitarian weapon for foot-soldier-to-foot-soldier confrontations, where lightweight weapons usually won).

Daggers are effective and easy to make. This old dagger apparently was made from an old file and fitted with a wooden handle that was wrapped with steel wire and painted black, creating a crude but undoubtedly effective weapon.

Likewise, the short span of American history during which swords, knives, and bayonets were actually being used in combat saw the relegation of heavy sabers to ceremonial use. Heavy knives like the Confederate D-Guard Bowie, the U.S. Marines' Entrenching Machete (a bolo-style knife used during both world wars) the Air Corps' Survival Machete (actually a large bowie), and so on were discarded or given away by troops interested only in their survival. By World War II, the dagger-shaped M3 and F-S Commando designs had become the fighting knives of choice, with the bowie style only regaining popularity when it was shrunk to the small proportions of the Ka-Bar. The truth of the matter is that those who actually use knives in combat on a regular basis adopt a short, lightweight design when it becomes available to them, and the style usually includes a narrow, pointed blade ideal for jabbing attacks that create maximum damage with minimum exposure to danger.

There are basically two types of small blades designed for a quick, jabbing attack that allows for reaching an enemy several feet away, severely wounding him, and then dropping back before he can deliver a counterattack. The most common is the dagger with a narrow, double-edged blade. Most modern combat daggers can trace their lineage to the period from 1300 to 1500 A.D. when Swiss, French, and Italian artisans starting adding double edges to their ornate weapons.

Another strong influence came from the Scottish dirk, which dates back to the 1550s,

and the *sqian dubh*, both of which drew more than their fair share of English blood and were later carried by immigrants to the United States in the 1700s.

Some of these early blades, especially those from Italy, were designed solely for combat, though nearly all could be used for fighting when the need arose. But like today's pocketknife, most early daggers were simply utility knives that rarely drew blood—a job the double-edged design does admirably when needed.

The dagger design is strong (an important point given some of the poor steels knifesmiths had to work with), but the same thick blade that doesn't break under the strains of fighting also has edges that aren't noted for their cutting abilities. So even today, those wanting a combat blade that can also chop wood or sever ropes with one swing need a bowie or machete, but those wanting a lightweight weapon that can quickly and quietly dispatch an enemy should reach for a dagger.

With modern steels, which are stronger than those of several centuries ago, it is possible to create a double-edged blade that can have an edge as good as most bowies. This is possible by doing away with some of the dagger's symmetry, avoiding the "double V" cuts to the two edges (so the cross section of the blade has a diamond shape). Then deep grinds can be made on either edge of one side of the blade while the other side is left flat or has a hollow concave cut added to it. This creates an edge that rivals that of the bowie while retaining the pluses in shape and light weight offered by the dagger layout. The addition of serrations on one or both edges provides an even more impressive cutting tool. While few knife makers currently are using the flat-side design or serrations, it seems probable that this will be the next step in this configuration of knife. Once this change is made, the dagger will become both an excellent fighting blade and a useful utility tool.

The stiletto is similar in concept to the dagger but lacks the sharpened twin edges. In effect, this weapon simply is a glorified ice pick. But like the dagger, it is easily concealed and highly effective when used in attacks to the back, chest, or—more rarely—spine and skull. These targets allow the stiletto's blade to reach vital organs, creating wounds that lead to shock or death.

Often, stiletto blades have triangular or quadrangular cross sections with three or four unsharpened edges, but this isn't a hard-and-fast rule. Such cross sections increase the strength of the blade while keeping its weight down and also increase the diameter of the wound they create.

The term "stiletto" has been corrupted by those passing antiknife laws as well as commercial sellers of (generally) Italian-made, thin-bladed, single-edged folding knives. While these knives operate like a stiletto in concept, they aren't true stilettos. Most of these knives have such narrow blades that they are unreliable in combat, often snapping off and leaving the user defenseless. Additionally, Hollywood has portrayed these knives as being weapons utilized by criminals, so getting caught with one in a pocket is not wise.

Some knife experts and makers, including Randall Knives, use the term stiletto to designate daggers with very narrow blades, but since this term can include blades with both sharpened and unsharpened edges, such usage creates more than a little confusion. While it's wise to be aware of these overlaps in terms, "stiletto" generally refers to a weapon with a narrow, pointed blade without sharpened edges (which is how it will be used in this book).

Most state and city governments outlawed the carrying of daggers (and often bowies) in laws dating back to the 1800s. For the most part, these laws have never been repealed, even though outlaws now carry equally illegal pistols or, as often as not, the knives that were supposed to be stamped out a century ago by these ineffective laws.

This has left the citizen who wishes to defend himself the choice of going unarmed or breaking the law. The catch-22 is that criminals often are not prosecuted for carrying concealed knives when they do have them, and in some areas, a citizen who isn't suspected of committing a crime simply may receive a reprimand (perhaps with his knife confiscated by the officer) and be turned away. This isn't a hard-and-fast rule, however, and it varies even within the same precinct. While a citizen with a concealed dagger under his expensive three-piece suit may get off free, the guy with a small plastic push dagger stuffed into the waistband of his worn jeans and concealed by his T-shirt may end up behind bars, even though both were equally innocent or guilty (depending on your point of view). While justice may be blind, law enforcement officers aren't, and citizens who look less well-off or appear to be criminals (because of their hair length or skin color) may have the book thrown at them.

And the book may even have rigged rules. In a few states, it is a misdemeanor to be caught with a loaded pistol concealed on the body without a permit to carry it, while the same person, if caught with a dagger or stiletto, will be charged with a felony. Again, being aware of the law is important before choosing a weapon.

The bottom line is that it's important to give some thought to possible consequences before deciding to carry a concealed dagger or stiletto. It's always wise to consult the city and state attorneys (not the local police) to verify what the laws really are and then to contact a local lawyer to determine whether or not and how often the regulations are enforced. Furthermore, some parts of the United States consider a knife locked in a car trunk or glove compartment to be a weapon concealed upon the person. Again, contacting the proper sources for information about the law can save a world of problems.

(It has been said that if a person has never been stopped and searched, he shouldn't worry about carrying a concealed weapon since it isn't likely that he will be stopped and searched at all. This makes some sense, but a person carrying an illegally concealed weapon only needs to be stopped and searched once or fail to conceal the weapon completely and draw unwanted attention. Then he's in really hot water.)

As mentioned earlier, in most areas of the United States, having a large dagger or stiletto for self-defense in the home is legal (though again, local laws must be checked). In such places, the knives covered in this chapter make ideal self-defense weapons, especially in areas where firearms may be hard to own legally. Additionally, because of the wide range of daggers and stilettos manufactured as well as the availability of antique versions of these knives, a homeowner can "collect" them and, when a criminal breaks in, be forced to use whatever's at hand to defend himself—in this case an effective dagger. (While this may not necessarily be a good legal defense, in many areas it likely will be.)

It should be noted, too, that some locales may grant a concealed-weapons permit that allows the carrying of a knife for self-defense. Those living in such an area might wish to pursue this, especially given the antigun sentiments currently in vogue, which might make a bureaucrat more apt to okay a knife than a gun. And in those in states and municipalities that allow carrying a blade for self-defense without a permit, it would be wise to get a copy of the law from the attorney general's office, photocopy it, and keep a copy in a billfold or purse so it can be shown to overzealous law officers who are often unaware of actual laws.

Their combat abilities and legal difficulties aside, daggers and stilettos offer some distinct advantages over other knives. Foremost is their ability to be concealed and their light weight. Where carrying a heavy bowie all day is a chore, most daggers on the belt go unnoticed by their owners.

The smaller size and lighter weight also translate into lower materials cost, and the edge of a dagger is not expected to be razor sharp, so manufacturers spend less time sharpening and honing the blade. This means daggers, when compared to folders or single-edged knives of equal quality, are normally much less costly. A dagger can be cast, have minimal polishing done to its blade, have a grip mounted to it (with this last step omitted in the case of daggers having wide tangs that act as handles), and it's ready to go. Even high-quality daggers usually carry reasonable price tags.

Because so many daggers and stilettos are selected for concealed carry, there is a wealth of special devices and sheaths available, with belt clips being the most common (holding the knife in position either vertically or horizontally in relation to the belt). Also available are special harnesses that hold the sheath on the belt diagonally (facilitating a quick draw from behind the back) or attach it to the forearm or leg (the former being practical for men with flappy jackets and the latter being practical for almost no one). There are harnesses for under-the-arm, pistol-style carry, and boot holsters, which may have been practical two hundred years ago but are sadly outdated now in this day of Nikes and tight pants worn outside boots.

While conveying a knife in a boot is a poor practice these days, the dagger that was developed in the 1800s for this type of carry is an ideal hideout blade since it generally is small, thin, and light. Perhaps the best known of these is Gerber's Mark I (designed by Al Mar when he was with Gerber). It is often found in the packs of pilots as well as on the webbing of SWAT team officers. It's light but capable of dealing with a hand-to-hand fight if the need arises.

Like Gerber's Mark II, the Mark I has a cast-aluminum handle with a black finish on its grip to aid in retention. It has a shape similar to the Mark II but shorter, lacking the conical end segment of the Mark II. The 5-inch stainless steel blade is double-edged; weight is 5.3 ounces and cost is around $50.

Gerber has a nearly identical knife marketed as the Command I. One of the edges of its 5-inch blade only extends halfway up and is serrated, giving it a bit better cutting ability than many other boot knives. The price is $50. The Guardian I from Gerber has a narrower 5-inch blade and more slender grip with abbreviated cross guard, giving it a lighter 4.2 ounce weight. Cost is $51. The Guardian II has only a 3.375-inch blade, a grip lacking cross guards, and a weight of 3 ounces. It costs $42.

The Clip Lock is an even lighter dagger offered by Gerber. This stainless steel knife has a 3.5-inch blade with a widened tang that acts as the grip. The knife can be released from its Zytel sheath by pressing a clip. It is available in two different blade styles—with serrations along an entire edge or only halfway up one edge. Cost is around $40.

The Brigada Paracaidista is nearly identical to the Mark I except for a blackened blade and one edge that has serrations down its entire length. Used by elite Spanish antiterrorist units, the dagger has a 5-inch blade and cast handle identical to the Gerber model. This knife is available from Atlanta Cutlery for $50.

Many cheap copies of the Mark I are also seen from time to time. These are best avoided given their inferior quality and the relatively low cost of the Gerber blade.

Puma offers its stag-handled Boot Knife with a 4.5-inch blade and a weight of 4.2 ounces. While the blade has a drop point similar to that of a bowie, its narrowness allows it to be utilized effectively for dagger-style fighting. Cost is around $130.

Ek has produced what appears to be a Mini-Ek in the form of its Secret Agent boot knife. The dagger has the standard Ek design with a double-edged blade that extends to a full tang. The Secret Agent usually is wrapped with black nylon parachute cord (as are some of the full-size Ek combat knives). It seems likely that other versions of this blade having the distinctive wooden "handprint" handles will be added to the company's line in the near future. The blade is 3.5 inches long and the knife weighs 3.2 ounces. It costs $60.

The Gryphon Utility/Boot knife, designed by noted knifesmith Robert Terzuola, has a 4-inch bowie blade, making it somewhat of an anomaly in boot knives. However, the false edge is sharpened about a third of the way along its spine lines. The Gryphon knife has a tough Zytel grip and cross guards molded around its tang. Cost is $150.

One sublime example of the boot knife is the SOG Pentagon. It has a rounded grip reminiscent of a Scottish dirk and both a standard and serrated edge on the 4.75-inch blade, giving it an added cutting power many daggers lack. The grip is black Kraton, which offers excellent purchase; so good, in fact, that the manufacturer has departed from the traditional style and left off the cross guard on this knife. The 5.2-ounce knife carries a price tag of around $80.

Although designed as a diver's knife, the Kershaw Amphibian also makes an excellent boot dagger and is even available with a leather sheath in addition to its ABS plastic diving sheath (which is actually a better choice above or below the water). One side of the double-edged 3.75-inch blade is serrated for added cutting capabilities. Cost is about $45.

Atlanta Cutlery offers a diver-style boot knife, the Skeleton Handle Dagger, that's simply a bar of stainless steel with a handle ground into one end and a sharp dagger blade on the other. Overall length is 8.25 inches, with 4.25 inches being sharpened blade. Cutouts in the grip make it easier to grasp and also lower the weight of the knife to only 2.5 ounces. Users wishing a more substantial grip can create one by wrapping nylon cord around the tang. The cost of the dagger is a bargain-basement $13.

In 1977, A.G. Russell introduced a knife called the Sting made of a single stainless steel forging. The blade and grip are molded into one solid piece. It continues to be popular today, with several additional versions offered, including one having wooden scale grips of rosewood or black rucarta, a black Teflon-finished model, one with a mirror polish, one with black chrome finish, and one with a nonreflective black finish. These have a 3.25-inch double-edged blade and sell for $50 to $60.

A Zytel plastic version of the Sting has also been created. Marketed as the CIA Letter Opener, it weighs less than an ounce. While the Zytel isn't as durable as steel, it is strong enough to be lethal, making it a handy weapon that can be carried and concealed in ways impossible with a standard dagger. Best of all, its $7 price tag makes it affordable.

Taking advantage of this same inexpensive plastic, Choate Machine & Tool has also created several "letter

The SOG Pentagon has a rounded grip and both a standard and serrated edge on the 4.75-inch blade. (Photo courtesy of SOG Specialty Knives)

openers" with dagger lines. They are marketed as the Executive Letter Openers, and undoubtedly more than a few have passed through metal detectors and boarded planes, carried by citizens interested in protecting themselves in airports not noted for their lack of crime. The Zytel daggers are extremely strong; Choate company literature boasts that the Executive Letter Openers can be driven through 1/2-inch plywood with minimum damage to the blade.

The Executive Letter Opener I was the first of the Choate plastic blades; the original version was white, but they now come in black like the company's other Zytel products. The Executive Letter Opener II has the same dimensions as the I but has a rounded grip (rather than rectangular) and a slightly narrower blade. Both have an overall length of 7.75 inches, with a 4.5-inch blade. Each version weighs only 2 ounces and costs a mere $4.50, making these discrete defensive blades light to carry and easy on the pocketbook.

Choate Machine & Tool's rectangular-handled Executive Letter Opener I (top) and curved Executive Letter Opener II (bottom) undoubtedly have bravely gone where other blades have failed to go thanks to their non-metal construction, which gives them a "stealth" design when it comes to metal detectors.

Choate Machine & Tool has also created a stainless steel version of the Executive Letter Opener II which is sold as the Stainless Steel Stinger, perhaps due to its close resemblance to the Al Mar Stinger. The Choate rendition has a black plastic handle and 4.5-inch stainless

steel blade. It is sold in an unsharpened condition for $11. (At the time of this writing, it appeared that production of the Choate Stinger may be discontinued, though the company still had a number of the knives in stock.)

In addition to the combat daggers like the S-F Commando, Silver Hawk, Applegate-Fairbairn, Ek, Gerber Mark II, and others mentioned in Chapter 2, there is a wealth of full-size dagger designs available on the marketplace. While these aren't as easily concealed as boot daggers, the full-size blades are better for combat since they offer added reach and more comfortable handles. This can be a big plus, especially for those who use the blades to defend themselves at home, where there is little or no need to keep the knife concealed.

One such dagger is Blackjack's Blackmoor Dirk, with a distinctive Kraton handle that looks like an elongated diamond, a steel cross guard, and a 6.125-inch double blade (with all the steel parts muted a dark gray). The Blackmoor has a thick spine running down the center of one side of its blade; the flip side, instead of being identical, as is the case with most daggers, has a hollow grind down its center. This allows the edges to be honed to a sharper finish. Blackjack also offers the Wasp, which is nearly identical to the Blackmoor but lacks a cross guard and has only a single sharpened edge. This version is designed for throwing but would also make an effective dagger. While some may dislike the feel of the pointy grip on these blades, they are sharp, tough daggers that are moderately priced in the $85 range.

Blackjack also offers the Tartan Dirk, which is nearly identical to the Blackmoor except for the blade length and finish. It has a longer 8.5-inch blade that is left "in the white" with the same hollow ground and the addition of serrations along its base, making it an effective cutter. Cost is $100.

Modern Combat Blades: The Best in Edged Weaponry

SOG's Patriot (Desert Dagger) has the distinction of being one of the few knives named after an antimissile system. (Photo courtesy of SOG Specialty Knives)

SOG's Patriot (Desert Dagger) has the distinction of being the first knife named after the antimissile system that performed so admirably during the Gulf War of 1991. The 9-ounce Patriot has a 6.5-inch double-edged blade with

Al Mar's Shadow I and Shadow IV are two excellent combat daggers with tough, Zytel grips. (Drawing courtesy of Al Mar)

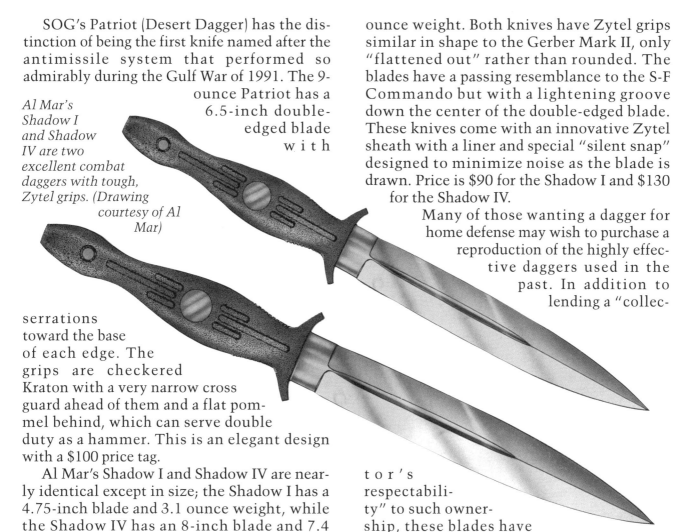

serrations toward the base of each edge. The grips are checkered Kraton with a very narrow cross guard ahead of them and a flat pommel behind, which can serve double duty as a hammer. This is an elegant design with a $100 price tag.

Al Mar's Shadow I and Shadow IV are nearly identical except in size; the Shadow I has a 4.75-inch blade and 3.1 ounce weight, while the Shadow IV has an 8-inch blade and 7.4

ounce weight. Both knives have Zytel grips similar in shape to the Gerber Mark II, only "flattened out" rather than rounded. The blades have a passing resemblance to the S-F Commando but with a lightening groove down the center of the double-edged blade. These knives come with an innovative Zytel sheath with a liner and special "silent snap" designed to minimize noise as the blade is drawn. Price is $90 for the Shadow I and $130 for the Shadow IV.

Many of those wanting a dagger for home defense may wish to purchase a reproduction of the highly effective daggers used in the past. In addition to lending a "collector's respectability" to such ownership, these blades have

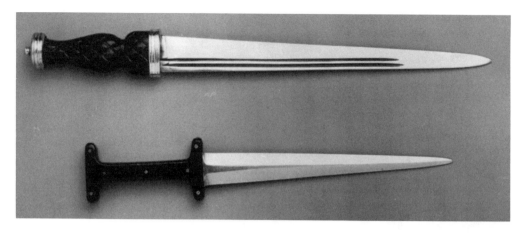

proven themselves to be deadly effective in actual fighting and, as such, are combat-proven designs.

Many such daggers are available from Atlanta Cutlery and its sister company, Museum Replicas Limited. Unlike some reproductions, which are simply wall hangers with brittle blades, these weapons are designed for theatrical and reenactment groups, and the blades are tempered to take a beating without breaking or bending. As such, they make excellent self-defense weapons if a little time is taken to add a sharp edge to them.

One such offering is patterned after the Scottish dirk. This weapon was first seen in the Scottish Highlands in the mid-1500s and is seen by many historians as the granddaddy of most American daggers, standing in about the same relationship to the modern dagger as the bowie knife does to the modern hunting knife. The dirk differs from the modern dagger in that it often has only one sharpened edge on its tapered blade. (The second edge is often plain or, on early examples, with teeth. This attempt to give the knife more utility eventually was abandoned because it was impractical—a lesson some modern knife designers need to take note of.) Sometimes the secondary edge on the dirk will have a short false edge or be embellished with a scroll pattern. The dirk's grip usually lacks a cross guard, and often has an ornate pommel.

The dirk otherwise appears nearly identical to the modern dagger, tapered blade and all. Like other ancient patterns made when human labor was cheap, dirks often display carved grips, etched blades, or other handiwork, and many are genuine works of art.

Museum Replicas Limited has two dirks that could easily be pressed into defensive service. One is the Bonny Scottish Dirk, with an 11.75-inch blade having one sharpened edge and a 5-inch false edge on its other side. The ebony handle on this beautiful knife is carved in a weave pattern with nickel silver studs. The flat pommel and minimal cross guard (which, as with most dirks, serves to keep the grip in place rather than protect the fingers) are matching nickel silver. It has an overall length of 17.5 inches and weighs 1 pound. Cost is $80.

The company's Early Scottish Dirk has a 13-inch single-edged steel blade with brass cross guard and pommel. This dirk weighs 14 ounces and its dark wood grip is carved in a diamond pattern. Cost is $125. Unlike most of the other blades in this chapter, the Early Scottish Dirk doesn't come with a scabbard, but an ornate one is available for an additional $44.

Museum Replicas also offers two Sword Hilted Daggers with 13-inch double blades and a choice of either steel or brass cross guards and pommels. Weighing 1 pound, 4 ounces each, these are no-nonsense daggers that resemble short swords; cost is $80 for either one. Similar in concept but lacking a large cross guard is the Baselard Dagger, a reproduction of a Swiss thirteenth-century dagger with a 10-inch blade. The grip, fastened to the tang, forms both the cross guard and mirror-image pommel to create a surprisingly comfortable grip. It costs $68. (The Baselard has the dubious honor of having been adopted as the pattern for the ceremonial dagger used by German Nazis during World War II.)

Atlanta Cutlery offers the Bahia Dagger, an

interesting reproduction of the Brazilian dagger from Bahia. This reproduction boasts a 6-inch stainless steel double-edged blade and an ornate turned handle of resin and nickel silver. Cost is $50.

Although it might be considered a short sword, the *Qama* has a double-edged blade that ends in a sharp point, giving it all the characteristics of a dagger. The design is believed to be modeled after the Roman short sword, and the grip is certainly similar to the parent weapon. The *Qama* continues to be carried—and used—in both Soviet Georgia and Iran. Atlanta Cutlery offers a model with water buffalo horn scales, 17.5-inch steel blade, and a metal-tipped wooden sheath with a leather cover. Made by the same India government contractor that manufactures the *kukri* blades, the cost is only $30.

Several areas of the world have produced combat blades that are nearly identical to the dagger except for the addition of curves to their double-edged blades. Such curves can act like serrations, giving the blade additional cutting power since more of the edge is exposed during a stabbing attack.

The most fearsome of these is the Philippines' *kris* dagger. Atlanta Cutlery offers an excel-

lent reproduction of this deadly design complete with a 12.5-inch wave blade. Weighing only 14 ounces, the knife has an overall length of 16.5 inches and comes with water buffalo horn grips and integral steel cross guard. Cost is $30.

The Arab *jambiya* is another time-honored blade that has the distinction of being the most widely carried knife in the world, being found in the hands of people from the Atlantic coast of Africa to the Indonesian islands. Its double-edged, daggerlike blade is curved similar to a scimitar blade but ends in a sharp point without flaring out. The grip is nearly the opposite of what is seen in the West; it is narrow in the middle and expands near the cross guard and at the pommel. It's also surprisingly comfortable and secure to hold. Atlanta Cutlery sells two models, the Yemeni Jambiya with a 8.75-inch blade and buffalo horn handle (for $50) and a Persian Jambiya with a 10-inch blade and horn handle ($28).

During the mid- to late-1800s, a blade that would appear to have been influenced by the Scottish dirk was the Arkansas Toothpick. It enjoyed less popularity than the bowie but was quite effective in its own right. This knife was as massive as a large bowie but had a double-edged, tapered blade ending in a point and usually a symmetrical handle. (It should be noted that some of the early bowies had similar spear-point blades, so it is possible that the Arkansas Toothpick is an offspring of the bowie.)

The Qama has a double-edged blade that ends in a sharp point and is believed to be modeled after the Roman short sword.

The kris dagger has curves on its double-edged blade that act in the same manner as serrations, giving the blade additional cutting power since more of the edge is exposed during a stabbing attack.

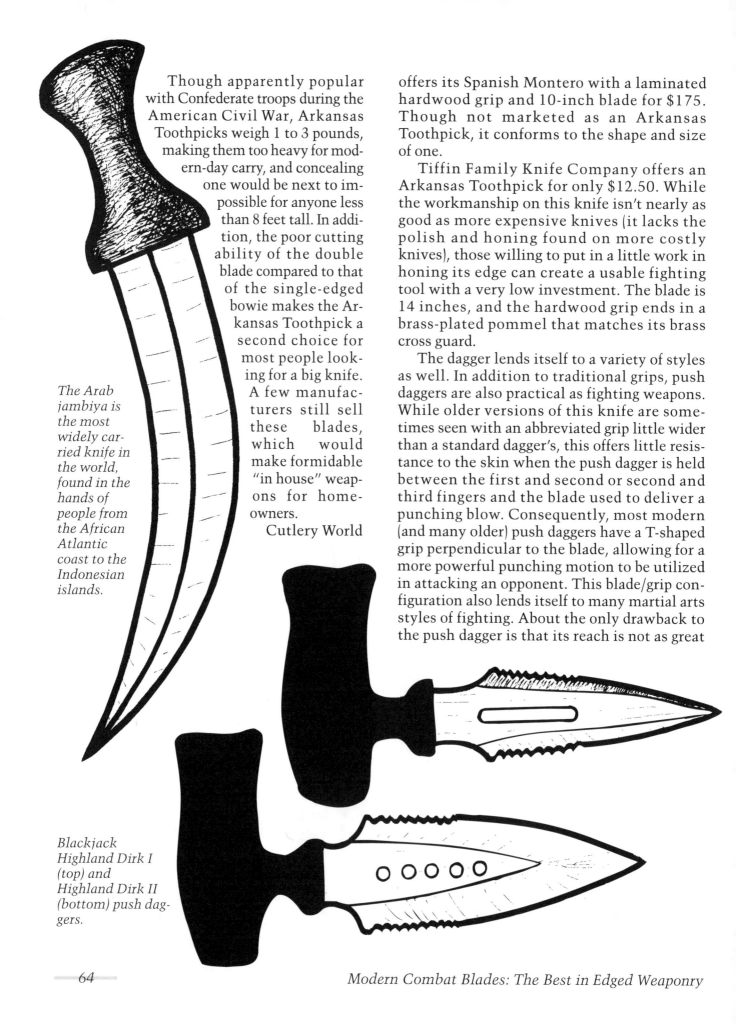

Though apparently popular with Confederate troops during the American Civil War, Arkansas Toothpicks weigh 1 to 3 pounds, making them too heavy for modern-day carry, and concealing one would be next to impossible for anyone less than 8 feet tall. In addition, the poor cutting ability of the double blade compared to that of the single-edged bowie makes the Arkansas Toothpick a second choice for most people looking for a big knife. A few manufacturers still sell these blades, which would make formidable "in house" weapons for homeowners.

Cutlery World

offers its Spanish Montero with a laminated hardwood grip and 10-inch blade for $175. Though not marketed as an Arkansas Toothpick, it conforms to the shape and size of one.

Tiffin Family Knife Company offers an Arkansas Toothpick for only $12.50. While the workmanship on this knife isn't nearly as good as more expensive knives (it lacks the polish and honing found on more costly knives), those willing to put in a little work in honing its edge can create a usable fighting tool with a very low investment. The blade is 14 inches, and the hardwood grip ends in a brass-plated pommel that matches its brass cross guard.

The dagger lends itself to a variety of styles as well. In addition to traditional grips, push daggers are also practical as fighting weapons. While older versions of this knife are sometimes seen with an abbreviated grip little wider than a standard dagger's, this offers little resistance to the skin when the push dagger is held between the first and second or second and third fingers and the blade used to deliver a punching blow. Consequently, most modern (and many older) push daggers have a T-shaped grip perpendicular to the blade, allowing for a more powerful punching motion to be utilized in attacking an opponent. This blade/grip configuration also lends itself to many martial arts styles of fighting. About the only drawback to the push dagger is that its reach is not as great

The Arab jambiya is the most widely carried knife in the world, found in the hands of people from the African Atlantic coast to the Indonesian islands.

Blackjack Highland Dirk I (top) and Highland Dirk II (bottom) push daggers.

Modern Combat Blades: The Best in Edged Weaponry

as that of a knife with a standard grip and the same blade length.

Push daggers date back to the 1800s, perhaps even farther back, and therefore can be found in antique stores as well as in sparkling new forms in dealer's catalogs. They are also favorites among custom knife makers, so more than a few beautiful renditions are seen in collector's display cabinets. (And, of course, the popularity of these knives has caused legislators to make them illegal in many areas, just as with standard daggers, so purchasers should check into local and state laws before carrying one.)

Blackjack offers two styles of push daggers, the Highland Dirk I and Highland Dirk II. The I weighs 3.4 ounces, has a narrower 4-inch blade, and costs around $35, while the II weighs 4.2 ounces, has a wider 4.5-inch blade, and costs about $40. Both have offset grips that fill the hand better but also necessitate drawing the knife and replacing it in the same manner to avoid an awkward "upside down" hold.

Cold Steel has two models of push daggers. The Defender I (originally called the

The Cold Steel Defender II.

Defender I is more practical for combat; the Defender II makes a better utility knife, however, and may appeal to those wanting a sharp cutting tool that can double as a last-ditch weapon. Cost is around $90 for the Defender I and $70 for the Defender II.

Atlanta Cutlery offers the Maverick, which is loosely styled after an 1800s push dagger with a wide grip covered with Pakkawood

The Cold Steel Defender I has a 3.75-inch spear-point blade.

Terminator—a name that undoubtedly didn't help owners who had to appear in court to justify using the blade for self-defense) has a 3.75-inch spear-point blade and 3.8-ounce weight. Originally called the Urban Skinner, Cold Steel's Defender II is similar to the I but has a 2.5-inch bowie-style blade and weighs 3.5 ounces. Both have Kraton grips.

With its longer, double-edged blade, the

scales, for $40. The stainless steel, double-edged blade is 4 inches long. Some users of this knife may wish to round off the sharp points at either end of the grooved grip; while these give it a "longhorn" look, the points can be uncomfort-

The Maverick push dagger sports wide "longhorn" grips.

able when the blade is worn and might also cause injury to the user.

Another push dagger, this one with a formidable 5-inch double blade, is offered by Atlanta Cutlery as the Total Recall. As the name suggests, it's modeled after the weapon in the sci-fi movie of the same name. Unlike most knives inspired by movies, this one would give good service in actual combat, making it both utilitarian as well as collectible. The wide, rubberized grip has finger swells and, as an added bonus, the knife comes with a versatile sheath that has loops for several styles of carry as well as a spring-steel clip for quick attachment to a belt or clothing. Cost is $37.

A third offering from Atlanta Cutlery is the Key Ring push dagger. The blade is formed of sheet metal with a quarter twist to create a joining point for its hollow grip (which has a screw-in cap that allows paper money or other small items to be carried in it). Of course, the other end has a ring for holding keys. The stainless steel, arrowhead-shaped blade is 1.75 inches long and double-edged. Cost is $12 complete with a leather sheath.

Choate Machine & Tool offers a lightweight, Zytel plastic version of the push dagger as its Ace of Spades. Weighing only 1.5 ounces, this tough blade can be carried in a pocket, serve as a key chain (thanks to a handy hole drilled in it), or even be worn under the clothing on a string around the neck—all virtually unnoticed by the owner or those around him. The double-edged blade ends in an arrowlike point and is 2 inches long. Cost is a mere $4.50.

The Executive Ice Scraper is a similar device offered by Choate. It, too, is made of tough black Zytel and weighs only 1.5 ounces. Rather than a sharp point, however, this version has a blade running down the length of its front, allowing it to create painful, but not life-threatening, wounds (a sort of pacifist's push dagger). While less effective than the other blades listed in this chapter, it does fill the niche between making a bare-handed response or a lethal response and may therefore appeal to some purchasers (and, yes, it will scrape ice off car windshields). It costs only $4.50.

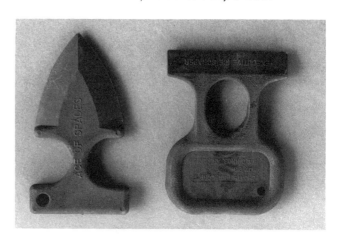

Choate Machine & Tool's Ace of Spades and Executive Ice Scraper are both lightweight and effective, thanks to their Zytel construction.

The Executive Ice Scraper is offered in more authoritative stainless steel and blue carbon versions. These can have their blades sharpened to a finer edge for greater cutting abilities (they're best not used on a windshield, however, since they may scratch it). Cost for the stainless steel version is $15.50, and the blued steel sells for $13. (At the time of this writing, it appeared that production of the Choate Stinger may be discontinued, though the company still had a number of the knives in stock.)

A similar wide-bladed cutting tool is mar-

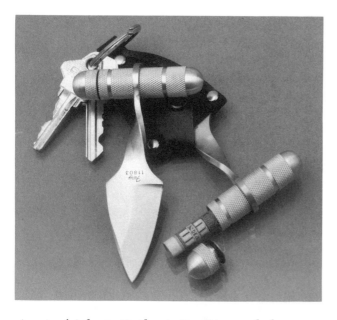

A pair of Atlanta Cutlery's Key Ring push daggers, one out of its sheath and the other with its hollow grip open to expose a roll of money. (Photo courtesy of Atlanta Cutlery)

Modern Combat Blades: The Best in Edged Weaponry

keted as the Survival/Rescue Tool with built-in wire stripper, bottle cap opener, and even a tile and glass cutter. The design of the Survival/Rescue Tool places four finger holes behind the blade, giving it a brass knuckle look; in fact, along with its metal construction, it would likely be considered brass knuckles by most courts of law. Given its inability to inflict more than superficial cuts during an attack, this blade is a second choice to either the "more legal" plastic versions of the Executive Ice Scraper or the much more effective knife designs discussed throughout this book.

Interestingly, the Eskimo culture has created a push dagger of sorts, the *ooloo*, with a wide, slightly rounded blade. It isn't used for combat, however, but as a tool for cutting and scraping animal hides. Custom knife makers occasionally create one of these blades which, like the Survival/Rescue Tool, are probably best passed over by those selecting a combat blade.

The likely forerunner of the dagger, the stiletto can vary in form from crude to a work of art. Any can be deadly, though those with edged blades (albeit unsharpened) are more effective than those which are simple pointed rods.

During the Middle Ages, the stiletto design was often used to give the coup de grace to a knight on the battlefield as well as by peasants interested in penetrating chain mail vests or getting a blade between armor plates. Three Middle Eastern styles of blade created for this purpose that are still carried today are the *choora*, the *pesh-kabaz*, and the similar *khanjar*, all of which have pointed blades with a T cross-section for added strength.

Unlike the true stiletto, these blades swell toward the grip and often are seen with the wider edge sharpened. In theory, the point of the blade would enter a link of mail, expanding and then breaking it as the blade widened. In practice, the weapon proved effective both on bare and mail-covered flesh.

A *choora* available from Atlanta Cutlery for $30 is a duplicate of those carried in Afghanistan. The 11.25-inch blade widens from a point to 1.5 inches at the grip. The company also offers the nearly identical Khyber with an 18-inch blade, making it more like a short sword than a stiletto. Cost is $37.

The modern-day "low men on the totem pole" of stilettos are the ice pick and its modern counterpart, the Phillips screwdriver. Because these are extremely cheap and common, however, they make ideal weapons for criminals or others wishing to have a blade that can be discarded after being used.

The big catch with ice picks and screwdrivers in self-defense use is that they can be very slow in stopping an opponent unless skill and luck come into play with a strike to a major organ. Otherwise, it may take hours or longer before an opponent is downed by internal bleeding from a counterattack with either of these weapons. (Ice-pick-style blades are often concealed in ink pens to create a last-ditch weapon. These and other concealed blades are covered in Chapter 12.)

During World War II, the Office of Strategic Services (OSS), the forerunner of CIA, created what has come to be known as a Sleeve Dagger. These were actually stilettos with an overall

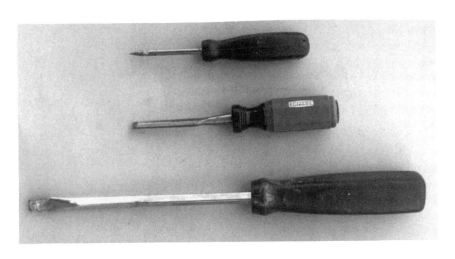

Stilettos are as close as the home shop. Shown here are three likely candidates: an ice pick/awl, small wood chisel, and long screwdriver.

The OSS Sleeve Dagger was a small stiletto capable of being hidden on the person of an agent, giving him a last-ditch combat blade that often escaped detection during a pat-down search.

length of 5 to 6 inches that could be hidden on the person in various locations, including, as the name suggests, in a sleeve sheath. Currently, the Cutlery Shoppe offers reproductions of these for $75 each. This rendition has an overall length of 7.25 inches with a 3.75-inch grooved spike blade.

A slightly refined version of the stiletto is manufactured by Pat Crawford and marketed as the Devil's Dart. It comes in two versions: a 3.5-inch-blade "Leg" version for carry in a leg sheath, and a 3-inch-blade "Arm" version for an arm sheath. Needless to say, the leg sheath is nearly impossible to use quickly, making the arm carry a better option. Cost is around $75 per Devil's Dart.

Pat Crawford has also created the Sharp Baton, an 18.5-inch aluminum baton with an end that unscrews to reveal a 5.75-inch flat stiletto blade. In theory, this gives the user the option of using either a blade or baton for self-defense; in practice, getting the blade unscrewed in time would probably be hard to do. Cost is $140.

Taking advantage of the inexpensive but strong Zytel plastic, Choate Machine & Tool has also created a stiletto as part of its Executive Letter Opener series. The Executive Letter Opener III has an overall length of 7.75 inches with a 4.5-inch ribbed blade. While this stiletto is not quite as tough as a steel blade, the weight is under 2 ounces, making it light to carry and easy to conceal. Cost is only $4.50.

Museum Replicas Limited has reproduced several Renaissance stilettos with patterns that were tested firsthand during Italian court intrigues and politics. Often found in the hands of assassin and defender alike, they have

proven themselves to be deadly effective. Both reproductions are made of high carbon steel and are heat treated to a strong spring temper. The larger of these has a 7.75-inch quadrangular blade that comes to a wicked point; it weighs 8 ounces and costs $55. The smaller has a 4.75-inch blade, weighs 5.5 ounces, and costs $48.

Do-it-yourselfers can create several inexpensive versions of the stiletto for very little money and with only a small amount of work. The 12-inch spike bayonet found on the SKS can be adapted into a long stiletto by simply adding a grip and sharpening its wide point. With SKS rifles being imported and modified to deer rifles,

Renaissance Italy produced some beautiful, if deadly, stilettos like these. These blades continue to be offered by Museum Replicas Limited.

Modern Combat Blades: The Best in Edged Weaponry

The 12-inch spike bayonet found on the Chinese SKS can be adapted into a long stiletto by simply adding a grip and sharpening its wide point.

it seems likely that many owners will have bayonets they'll want to sell or trade for very little.

In many college towns with fencing teams, old fencing foils are available for a song. These can have their blades cut to any length under 35 inches and pointed with a file. The pommels on these generally unscrew, making it easy to remove the bell-shaped finger guards and replace them with more conventional grips. Of course, any length of rod—whether wooden, metal, or plastic—can be pointed to create an improvised stiletto for anyone needing a weapon in a hurry.

• • • • •

Whether of an antique design or made of space-age Zytel, daggers and stilettos remain effective weapons that will likely be in the hands of citizens and professional soldiers alike for many decades and probably centuries to come. That can be said of very few of mankind's inventions.

Chapter 6
SAMURAI BLADES

U nfortunately, the Japanese "banzai" charges of World War II, transmogrified by fictional accounts and war stories and coupled with the rash of Oriental martial arts films in the 1970s and 1980s (with spin-offs featuring everyone from Chuck Norris to Teenage Mutant Ninja Turtles), have glorified the Eastern styles of fighting without showing their shortcomings.

War myths and the silver screen have created modern legends that many people accept as fact. Otherwise credible individuals tell, with straight faces, tales of Japanese Imperial soldiers slashing barrels off machine guns with one flick of a sword and assure those within earshot that such a swordsman has no equal, regardless of the weaponry others may possess.

But the truth is different.

In reality, the Japanese rarely used their swords or bayonets decisively in combat during World War II except to slaughter prisoners, kill wounded, or commit suicide when cornered by Allied troops. While the picture of a swordsman being able to hold his own against modern weaponry is a romantic ideal, it isn't factual.

Westerners also often fail to recognize that Oriental cultures—especially the Japanese during the feudal period, when samurai swords and other weapons were actually in use—were stagnant, closed societies in which even the patterns of weapons were determined by the emperor and never modified or changed to any extent. The weapons were perfected *within* these design parameters, and weapons techniques were polished to perfection, but being able to best an opponent armed with a similar weapon (or slice through an unarmed peasant, as often as not) didn't mean that the swords and other bladed weapons were any better than those developed in the Middle East, Europe, and the Americas.

During the height of the Japanese feudal system of the Samurai Era (835-1867 A.D.), the bladed weapon became the "soul of the samurai" and was steeped in legend and ceremony. Interestingly, the samurai warriors called all

The wakizashi is similar to other traditional Japanese swords but generally has a handier 17-inch blade.

their bladed weapons "swords" regardless of length; thus, the short knifelike *tanto* meant, literally, "half sword." Blade length was often measured by the *shaku*, which equals 11.93 inches.

The actual long sword of the samurai was very effective within the confines of the culture. But, like the European sword, the Japanese blade soon fell to the wayside in military use when firearms were introduced.

Some of the shorter-bladed Japanese weapons can be pressed into service as credible defensive weapons. As with most European swords, however, the longer Oriental swords are not ideal for modern combat due to the low ceilings and narrow hallways found in most modern structures. Unless a person lives in a castle or needs a blade for outdoor use, long swords are just too cumbersome for consideration in a realistic assessment of defensive needs.

There is a wide variety of single-edged Japanese swords all based on similar patterns. These were often carried in sets by samurai warriors who, by law, were the only ones allowed to wear a combination of blades. Today these are most commonly sold in pairs for mounting on walls or stands. While antique Japanese swords vary considerably in length, newer sets usually come with a sword having a longer, 40-inch blade generally known as the *katana* (the "long sword," also called a *daito* or a *tachi*). The shorter sword in such sets is known as a *shoto* ("short sword," with 28-inch blade) or slightly shorter *wakizashi*, with a 17-inch blade.

When the samurai were actually carrying these weapons, most fighting was done with the *katana*, while the short sword was only used occasionally as a secondary weapon. Its principal purpose was the performance of ritualistic suicide, *seppuku* (also known as the "belly cut," or *hara-kiri*).

During the Japanese feudal period, master swordsmiths were popular figures. The cross guard, or *tsuba*, a small subcross guard called the *fuchi*, and the *kashira*, or pommel, were works of art in themselves. *Menuki*, tiny ornaments wrapped into the silk cords of the grip, held secret meanings known only to the owner of the blade. A small throwing knife, the *kozuka*, often was hidden in the scabbard and was used to penetrate the eyeholes of the armor worn into battle. The samurai fighting protocol allowed the *kozuka* to be used only in attacks against the eyes, throat, forehead, or wrists of an enemy.

By the end of the feudal period, an elaborate set of rules and etiquette was composed around the samurai sword itself. The blades were placed on ceremonial stands (*katanakake*) when not in use, and the scabbard went untouched by any but the owner of the sword. Those who did touch the scabbard of another samurai committed a serious breach of etiquette that led to a fight to the death. Swordsmiths often tested their swords by seeing how well they cut or disemboweled prisoners, carefully noting the effectiveness of the blade with inscriptions.

The blades of most Japanese swords are slightly curved, and all but the *wakizashi* have grips that accommodate two-handed use. What has become popular as the "ninja" *to* sword is similar to the *shoto* but has a shorter blade (around 23 inches long) and very little, if any, curve.

Of all the variations of these swords, the *wakizashi* and *to* could arguably be useful in modern-day combat, though the curved blade of the *wakizashi* makes jabbing attacks—useful in close-quarter fighting—somewhat awkward. The other Japanese swords are just too heavy and long to be anything but awkward in a confined area. For those wanting a long combat blade of modern manufacture, Cutlery Shoppe and Collector's Armory offer stainless steel *wakizashi* and other reproductions of

Modern Combat Blades: The Best in Edged Weaponry

samurai swords for as little as $112. Unlike many production "wall hangers," these swords come sharpened and have a tang running well into the pommel, making them strong enough for actual combat.

Oddly enough, the most suitable Japanese blade for modern combat is the *tanto*, which originally performed as a last-ditch weapon, utility knife, or ceremonial blade. Enemies defeated in combat were often beheaded with this blade and the head carried back to a superior (literally a "head man") so the samurai would be officially credited with having defeated an enemy. There are several forms of these short blades; the best known is the *tanto* (the "half sword," which is usually seen with a cross guard) and the *aikuchi* (which usually lacks a cross guard on its curved blade). Neither of these was considered a primary weapon, at least not until the designs became popular in the United States.

The man deserving credit for elevating the *tanto* into a combat weapon is Lynn Thompson, a former real estate salesman who gave up a thriving business to turn his love of knives into a business. His company, Cold Steel, started operation in 1981, marketing small push daggers that doubled as key rings. These created both the capital and business base to launch the introduction of a knife Thompson had been interested in for some time. He saw the *tanto* as a good candidate for a combat weapon, capable of withstanding strains which would snap the point off Western-style daggers and also capable of taking and maintaining a razor edge.

When Cold Steel's Tanto was introduced in the mid-1980s, industrial insiders thought the public would refuse to purchase such an expensive "oddball" blade. In fact, an aggressive ad campaign coupled

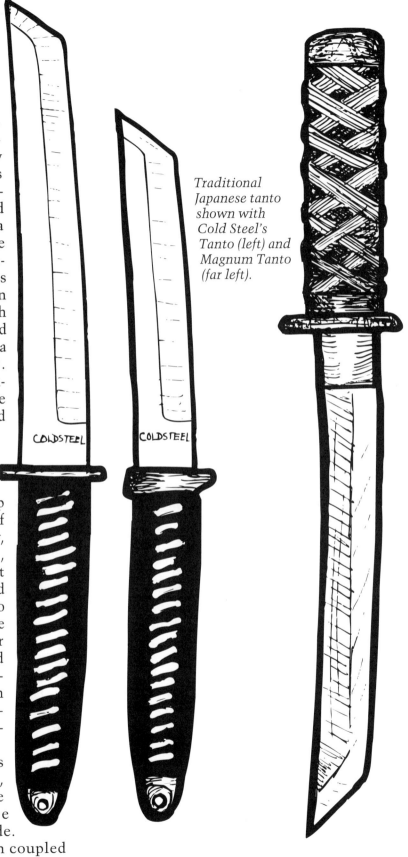

Traditional Japanese tanto shown with Cold Steel's Tanto (left) and Magnum Tanto (far left).

Samurai Blades

with the strength of the knife, its high quality, and—as luck would have it—a craze in the United States for Oriental-style martial arts equipment, made sales skyrocket. Cold Steel was selling the blades as fast as its Japanese subcontractors could fashion them. Other knife manufacturers, perhaps begrudgingly, have since added *tanto*-style blades to their offerings.

As is so often the case with designs adopted and adapted by the cross-pollination of cultures, the *tanto* that came across the Pacific was altered to make it into a better weapon. It lost most of its cross guard and had its traditional string and wood grip replaced with checkered Kraton to aid retention (becoming the first knife to use this rubberized material for a grip). Its blade was given a handy 5.75-inch length, with the knife weighing only 9.6 ounces. The *tanto* in Cold Steel's rendition became a fighting knife similar in concept to the bowie, suited to a slashing attack, while having a much tougher blade than most Western blades of similar size.

The Cold Steel Tanto didn't compromise on strength in the blade or the full tang that extends out the rear of the grip (where a lanyard hole is added). It is a tough knife that, as ads showed, could actually be pounded through a car door without damage to the knife. Even with a price tag of $150 (considerably higher than many bowies and other combat knives), the new Tanto sold well.

The success of its original Tanto led Cold Steel to create other models of the blade. Among these were the longer Magnum that was soon replaced by a refined Magnum II with a wider cross guard (more in keeping with the original Japanese *tanto* design), a 7.5-inch blade, a weight of 11.2 ounces, and a price of $250. A second version of the original Tanto was also created and marketed as the Special Ops Tanto, having a stainless steel cross guard and pommel cap like that of the Magnum II rather than brass as with the original Tanto. This new version costs $190.

While the Tanto series of knives are strong and have edges that come from the factory honed to a razor edge, Thompson recently decided to adopt the Japanese practice of lam-inating dissimilar steels to create a blade with a strong edge and flexible center to prevent breakage. This type of lamination was incorporated into a second series of *tantos* modeled after the first but having San Mai III laminated steel in their blades rather than stainless steel.

The basic knife in this group is the Master Tanto (otherwise identical to the Tanto and with a price tag of $200), the Master Ops Tanto (modeled after the Special Ops; $240), and the Magnum II-San Mai III (a mouthful of a name) that was created around the Magnum II design for $250.

To cut into the folder market, Cold Steel also created a series of *shinobu* folders with Kraton handles and *tanto*-style blades of San Mai III. The three models include the small Shinobu (with 1.75-inch blade and weighing 0.8 ounce), the medium (2.625-inch blade, 2.2 ounces), and the large (3.5-inch blade, 4.4 ounces). Of these, the large Shinobu ($90) might be employed as a defensive knife, though the blade length would make it marginal. Conversely, this knife could be carried legally in many areas of the United States while most of the other blades in this chapter couldn't without a special permit. Addition of the One Arm Bandit (described in Chapter 3) would enable the user to open the Shinobu quickly.

Other "Americanized" *tanto* designs are being imported into the United States, but most are similar only in appearance to Cold Steel's version and are inferior in terms of strength; they often snap off at the tang or blade when put under stresses that the Cold Steel blades survive. Consequently, for those looking for a serious fighting knife, it is best to choose the original, quality blades offered by Cold Steel.

For those wanting a slightly less expensive folder with a longer blade than offered by Cold Steel, Camillus carries a quality knife with a 4-inch, razor-sharp, *tanto*-style blade called the Promaster Tanto. It comes with Kraton scales on its grips to provide a sure purchase. Weight is 4.5 ounces, and cost is only $20. Like most other lockback folders, its capabilities can be enhanced with the addition of a One Arm Bandit stud to its blade.

• • • • •

While the long Japanese sword is as obsolete today as the European long sword, the shorter swords and especially the *tanto* designs are ideal for combat. The versions offered by Cold Steel and Camillus give users a quality knife with a strong, razor-sharp blade.

Chapter 7

THE KUKRI

ne of the few Eastern combat knives that has created a name for itself worldwide is the *kukri*, conceived by the Nepalese and carried by Gurkha tribesmen in the employ of the British military. The *kukri* is a relatively new weapon; the oldest-known specimens date back only as far as the 1600s. From the 1700s on, the pattern has remained pretty much as it is today, with minor variations brought about by the many craftsmen who make these blades as well as the variety of steels (varying from jeep leaf springs and sheet metal to high carbon steel) utilized to create the *kukri*.

The blades that are believed to have inspired the basic *kukri* design are as old as the knife is new. While it is hard to determine with any certainty, it appears the precursor of the *kukri* was the Egyptian *khepesh*, created well into the Iron Age when knife designers discovered that adding a curve or angle to a blade would increase its cutting abilities (which was important, given the poor edge-holding qualities of early knives and swords).

Most scholars feel the *khepesh* led to the Greek *kopis* of the fifth century B.C., a slashing sword featuring a forward curving blade like that of the *kukri*. About three times larger than the *kukri*, the *kopis* enabled Alexander the Great's troops to conquer the known world. Later, the Roman cavalry adopted a similar blade, undoubtedly influenced by the earlier Greek design. Because of the Roman Empire's close proximity to India, it is believed that this blade eventually was carried into the region, influencing the shapes of several popular Indian swords.

The Indian design apparently was introduced into Nepal by Rajput soldiers that invaded the area in the early 1300s, consolidating the tribes of the region into what was eventually to become Nepal. These invaders brought with them the weapons that inspired the creation of the *kukri* shortly after they arrived.

The Nepalese military was armed with swords, principally the *kora* and India *ram dao*, as well as the then new *kukri*, for some time, but the swords fell to the wayside with the introduction of firearms. Unlike the swords, the *kukri* remained at the side of the Nepalese since they had discovered it was both an excellent utility tool that citizens and soldiers alike could use on a day-to-day basis as well as a matchless fighting instrument when the need arose.

After bloody fighting between Nepalese soldiers and the East India Company (which was created to run English businesses in British colonies) in the 1800s, the British were so impressed with the savage abilities of the Gurkha tribe that the final peace treaty included the stipulation that the English military could recruit Gurkha troops into service with the East India Company. This arrangement has lasted to the present time, with Gurkha soldiers displaying amazing prowess in combat during World War I in Gallipoli, France, the Suez, and Mesopotamia; during World War II in Italy, Burma, and Northern Africa; with United Nations forces in the Congo; in border wars between India and China; in Southeast Asia, including Malaya, Borneo, Brunei, and Indonesia; and most recently in the Falkland Islands. Throughout this combat, the Gurkhas have established a reputation as ruthless fighters, often battling enemies hand-to-hand with the *kukri* blade and taking a heavy toll. With such success, it is little wonder that the knife they carried has also earned a reputation as being a deadly weapon.

(One U.S. Army unit also used *kukris* during World War II. The 5307 Composite Unit "Merrill's Marauders," operating behind Japanese lines in Burma, was resupplied by the British, and many *kukris* ended up in American soldiers' hands when the trading and swapping that occurs between troops had died down. Apparently these served principally as utility knives in the jungle, though it's possible a few drew enemy blood.)

Interestingly, unlike many other edged weapons that demand special fighting styles of their owners, the *kukri* doesn't. It is simply employed for various odd jobs on a day-to-day basis until its Gurkha owner becomes so familiar with it that he knows its capabilities and

Kukris come in a bewildering number of shapes and sizes, though they are generally easy to recognize thanks to a distinctive sloped blade.

uses it almost without thinking, resulting in near instinctive employment of the *kukri* in combat. The Gurkhas don't engage in any complicated training or have any schools teaching martial arts skills; there is no fancy footwork or complicated moves. The Nepalese fighter just draws his weapon and strikes his enemy much as a person might lash out with his fist.

Most Nepalese users of the *kukri* do employ a special cutting stroke that gives the blade extra momentum that creates a greater cut

Modern Combat Blades: The Best in Edged Weaponry

than it might otherwise. This is done by holding the knife loosely on the lifting windup before delivering a blow so the spine of the blade drops back almost even with the forearm. As the hand pulls the weapon toward its target, a snapping motion throws the blade forward with increased speed for added momentum. This translates into a powerful, often devastating slash.

Very large ceremonial *kukris* are made and issued one to a Gurkha regiment. These weigh more than 4 pounds and are often 2.5 feet long. Fighting *kukris* are considerably smaller, and, since the knives are handmade, there is a wide variety of styles and sizes. Even military versions of the blade show a wide diversity. But except for the ceremonial versions of the knife, most have blades from 10 to 14 inches, a forward curving or forward angled blade with the cutting edge on the lower forward region, and the widest part of the blade from just under 2 inches to about 2.5 inches. Blade surfaces vary from no adornment to fine engravings but generally have at least a lightening cut running down the first third of the blade on the sides along the spine.

Another feature that is usually present (except on blades made in a hurry during wartime supply efforts) is the half circle/ notch cutout, usually on the forward edge of the blade ahead of the grip. This embellishment apparently serves no actual purpose, and its original meaning seems to have been lost in antiquity. Among the theories as to its symbolic meaning are that it is there to remind the user to draw blood whenever it is unsheathed (this is likely Western hogwash since the blade is used for chores, regularly removed from the scabbard and replaced many times during the day), that it represents a guard to capture enemy blades (a near impossibility given the fact that the blade would have to be held backward at a steep angle to accomplish this), and that it represents the clitoris of the Hindu goddess Kali (no comment). No doubt it's just a matter of time before someone suggests it is there for use as a wire stripper. The fact is, no one— Nepalese bladesmiths, historians, or knife experts—understands why the notch is placed

on the blade. Today it's there simply because that's how it's always been made.

The handle of the *kukri* can be any of a wide range of materials, with wood being the most common. Horn, metal of all types, bone, ivory, or even jade are seen from time to time. With wooden handles, a single ring sticks out about midway up the grip. Like the notch on the blade, this serves no apparent purpose, and most users find the grip considerably more comfortable to use if this band is removed with a chisel or rasp. Most grips also swell out at the base. This makes the knife easier to retain, but the rear swelling at the base of the grip juts into the user's hand, making it uncomfortable with extended chopping. Therefore, rounding off the lower rear edge of the grip with a grinding wheel or file can make a big improvement in the feel of the *kukri*.

The scabbard on these knives is also seen in a wealth of configurations. The most common is wood with a leather covering. Usually at least two smaller pockets are incorporated into the design; these carry two tiny knives (usually very crude) or a small knife and a sharpening iron. Occasionally, whole tool kits are found in the sheath with screwdrivers, awls, and other odds and ends.

Within these design parameters there's a wide range of variation, including an "oddball" handle or blade found from time to time. Most Gurkha units have had their own variations of the blade, and *kukris* made for civilians show considerable variety.

The basic *kukri* design is very strong, and it is rare that a blade actually breaks. Therefore, purchasers of these knives can simply shop for cost and be prepared to do some sharpening (less expensive versions generally are sold without much of an edge ground into them) and some work grinding off the rear swell on the grip. About the only versions of the *kukri* that should be avoided are the highly polished, engraved (and sometimes even chromed) blades made in India for the tourist trade.

The best source for inexpensive, military-grade *kukris* is Atlanta Cutlery, which offers several different styles, including a military-issue *kukri* with a 12-inch blade (for $24), an officer's *kukri* with 9.5-inch blade ($26), an

Assam Rifles *kukri* (issued to the Gurkhas' special rifleman unit) with 13.5-inch blade ($26), and a British Gurkha regiment *kukri* with high carbon steel and 9.5-inch blade that is identical to those made for the British government ($30). The company also offers a huge ceremonial *kukri* with a 22.5-inch blade for $80.

All the *kukris* offered by Atlanta Cutlery have wooden handles except for the officer's *kukri* and the British Gurkha regiment model, which have buffalo horn grips. Fit and finish are fairly good, though the blades on each need some serious sharpening, as do the blades on the pair of companion knives nestled within the sheaths. But these are excellent buys that give the purchaser a quality combat blade of proven capabilities as well as a utility knife capable of handling the chores of a large knife or even an ax.

While one might argue that the inexpensive *kukri* that serves the Gurkhas so well should be good enough for most other users, there are American-made versions of the blade that carry price tags five to ten times higher than the standard versions. None of these, despite better quality, exhibit notably better cutting abilities than the original, though their handles are considerably more comfortable to use thanks to modern materials, and some of them have stainless steel blades, making them ideal for areas with high humidity or other environ-

Military-issue kukri offered by Atlanta Cutlery comes complete with a wood-covered leather sheath and two utility blades. The low price tag and nearly indestructible construction make it a very good buy.

ments that promote rust. The American blades generally hold an edge better than the Indian/Nepalese-made knives.

One of the American versions of the *kukri* is the Blackjack Reinhardt Combat *kukri* designed by noted bladesmith Hank Reinhardt. The 13.5-inch blade is made of a special alloy of stainless steel, said to retain an edge well while still remaining flexible. The knife has a Kraton grip that aids in retention and absorbs some of the impact shock of blows. Best of all, the shape of the handle makes it considerably more comfortable than the knife's namesake. The Combat *kukri* is available from Atlanta Cutlery for $150.

Cold Steel has also created a version of the *kukri*, the ATC (All-Terrain Chopper), featuring a tough 12-inch blade and Kraton handle. Unfortunately, the grip flares out at the rear, something some users may find uncomfortable. But for those who aren't bothered by it, the ATC has all the high-quality features Cold Steel is known for. Cost for the 23-ounce knife is $220.

Al Mar features the Pathfinder *kukri*. Unlike other Americanized versions of this blade, the Pathfinder has a less pronounced downward curve. Many users who find the blade of the standard *kukri* awkward to use (and some do) may prefer this one. Its less acute angle, along with its sharpened upper edge, would allow a thrusting attack, a capability that is only marginally present—if at all—with other versions of this knife.

The Pathfinder's handle is grooved Zytel with a machete style for added retention. It

*An
Americanized version of the kukri
marketed by Blackjack as its Reinhardt Combat
kukri, designed by noted bladesmith Hank Reinhardt.*

also has a cross guard, not found on most other versions of the *kukri*. With a 14-inch blade and 23.7-ounce weight, the $225 Al Mar Pathfinder offers a slightly different configuration of the *kukri* that may appeal to many buyers, especially those not interested in the conventional *kukri* design.

Becker Knife & Tool Corporation has created two versions of the *kukri*, which it markets as the Machax. They have 9.5-inch blades with full-tang grips and plastic scale handles. The standard Machax weighs 19 ounces and costs

$83, while the Warrior Machax with a sharpened false edge weighs 16.5 ounces and costs $90.

• • • • •

Whether an Americanized version of the knife or traditionally styled, the *kukri* is a powerful cutting tool and fine weapon. With the wide range of styles and prices available, those interested in a large, downswept blade are almost guaranteed that somewhere there is a *kukri* that will be just right for them.

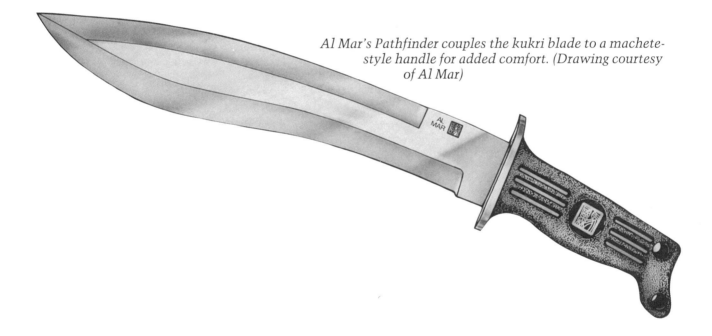

*Al Mar's Pathfinder couples the kukri blade to a machete-
style handle for added comfort. (Drawing courtesy
of Al Mar)*

Chapter 8
THE MACHETE

The machete is another of the relatively few modern combat blades that has the distinction of being popular worldwide in several nearly identical forms. The Philippines has a slightly heavier version of what is known as the machete in the Americas called the *bolo*, which has a rounded swell toward the end of the blade. In Africa, the *panga* is a nearly identical weapon, while the cutlass is the form the blade takes in the Caribbean and Guyana coast of South America. Even the Chinese created a similar weapon: the "butterfly knife," often seen in martial arts demonstrations as well as in the hands of combatants in Hong Kong and elsewhere. A short version of the machete was even aboard American space vehicles on lunar missions.

Like the kukri, the machete is seen in a bewildering number of shapes and sizes. This "homemade" machete has a large wooden handle and an oddly shaped tip— but it still gets the job done.

While it's doubtful that all these weapons developed along the same lineage, it seems likely that many of them developed from the cutlass that was popular among European navies during the eighteenth and nineteenth centuries. Richard F. Burton, in *The Book of the Sword*, suggests that the cutlass came to Europe by way of the Turkish scimitar, which often lacked a cross guard and had a top-heavy end to its blade in order to maximize its cutting power.

Some early cutlasses had long grips that enabled the user to add the power of a two-handed grip to his blows. But this was gradually replaced with a single-hand grip, often with a bell-style guard surrounding it, which protected the user's hand from enemy blades and enabled him to deliver a blow with the hilt at extremely close quarters. The weapon proved to be more effective than longer swords on the rolling, often crowded decks of ships, and was especially ideal for repelling boarders. Eventually the cutlass was displaced by firearms, but by that time it had traveled around the world and its design had been adopted as a tool by those who had seen its effectiveness.

the old ones having been worn out by continuous use of previous owners.

Today's machete is more apt to be seen cutting brush, trimming shrubs, or handling similar mundane tasks than being used in combat. This has the advantage of making the blade available for self-defense even in areas with restrictive governments that otherwise have disarmed the public—something many citizens of Third World countries have taken advantage of.

The lack of tempering and the ready availability of scrap steel for constructing machete blades keep the price of most of these tools under $20; those willing to put up with a cheap sheath can purchase one for under $10. The machete is truly the best bargain to be found in the way of combat blades.

The influence of the cutlass can still be seen in many of today's machetes. The small hole in the blade allows it to be hung on a nail.

Although today the name of the weapon varies from place to place, the machete basically has the same configuration worldwide, with a single-hand grip and a wide, thin blade. The blade usually isn't highly tempered since it is often created from all types of steel, including truck leaf springs and other scrap metal. Likewise, a wide variety of shapes, sizes, and materials is seen with grips. Undoubtedly, the invention of rolled steel—which made possible the creation of a blade by simply cutting the shape into the metal with a hacksaw or similar tool—spurred the popularity of these blades around the world, especially in areas where manpower is cheap and resources scarce.

The lack of a hard temper makes the blade go dull quickly. Consequently, many users have a mill bastard file tucked away in a sheath or backpack for sharpening the edge from time to time. On the flip side, the lack of hard temper and the width of the blade make the machete indestructible with normal use. Ancient blades often are capable of service with another generation of users with the addition of new grips,

The light weight, coupled with the thinness of the blade, makes the machete capable of cutting deeply with only a mild blow even more efficiently than most swords and bowie knives. Any time a fighter uses a machete, there will be serious mayhem and a strong possibility of severed limbs. The length of blades on machetes varies from 1 to 3 feet, but for actual combat in urban areas, 12 to 18 inches is ideal since longer blades tend to be unwieldy and collide with ceilings and walls indoors.

There are several important design features that wise buyers should check for before carrying one of these blades. Because the tool is often used like an ax or scythe, it's essential that the grip secures the machete to the hand, even when the palm is sweaty. To do this, the forward base of the grip should widen outward to help retain the tool, even when the hand is slightly relaxed. This has the added benefit of allowing the user to relax his grip as the blade collides with its target, thereby lessening the strain to the muscles and ligaments in the hand and arm. This can minimize the stress of cutting considerably and translates into fewer blisters and aching muscles at the end of a day of work. (And, as with the *kukri*, those who spend a lot of time becoming familiar with this tool will be able to wield it more effectively in combat.)

While the machete is principally a cutting blade, those who may be using it as a defensive weapon should choose a version with a slightly pointed tip to allow thrusting should it be called for. This also necessitates a grip with a cross guard, or a "D"-style grip. Plastic grips generally are more durable than wooden grips.

Traditionally, machetes manufactured by Collins were chosen by those using one on a day-to-day basis. But most of today's mass-produced machetes are as good as the Collins products, so there is no need to search for one of these often prized blades.

Brigade Quartermasters offers an excellent machete with a 12-inch blade marketed as the Worldwide Survival Tool. This machete—promoted by H. Morgan Smith, who founded the U.S. Air Force Tropic Survival School along with the training programs of several other countries—is nearly identical to those used to cut sugar cane in many areas and to the one carried by American astronauts on lunar missions. (W.R. Case & Sons Cutlery has created several commemorative versions of the astronaut's white-handled, saw-toothed knife; these are for collectors, however, and the $120 asking price for the limited number made would buy ten or more "common" machetes that would be every bit as good in terms of serviceability.)

Weighing only 12 ounces, the Worldwide Survival Tool is capable of holding its own against many bowie-style knives weighing two or three times more, and its cost of $10 is only a fraction of that of the more expensive knives. The light weight and low cost make it a good choice over many others. Brigade Quartermasters also offers an excellent Commando Jump Sheath that is a must for this machete, to

protect the blade as well as protect the user from getting accidental cuts. Cost is $14.

A tough "family" of similar machetes is offered by Brigade Quartermaster as the

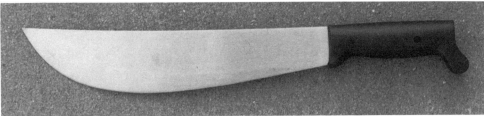

Brigade Quartermasters' excellent Worldwide Survival Tool has been promoted by survival expert H. Morgan Smith.

Sportsman Machetes. Each has a heavy plastic "D" grip that surrounds the fingers to help keep the weapon from slipping out of the hand as well as offering protection to the hand when cutting brush. The blade has a small hole drilled into it near the grip, which allows the machete to be hung on a nail in a closet or almost anywhere, waiting to be snatched up in a hurry should the need arise. For outdoor carry, a leather sheath is available; cost is $14 for an 18-inch sheath and $12 for a 12-inch.

There are two blade lengths of the Sportsman Machetes: an 18-inch blade (costing $15) and a 12-inch version (costing $14). A sawback version of the 12-inch blade is also offered for $20. While the blade is long and thin enough to make a saw blade viable—unlike with most combat knives—great care has to be taken to avoid having the fingers slip onto the blade, which lies with its edge pointed upward during such work. Generally, it's a safer bet to use the machete's ability to chop rather than depend on a sawback to do cutting chores. A folding saw carried in a pouch would add more weight to a user's load but would provide a greater degree of safety and make a better saw if the need for one arose.

The Army machete with a plastic handle riveted to an 18-inch parkerized steel blade is also available from Brigade Quartermasters at a cost of only $13. A heavy plastic sheath (military surplus and of high quality) goes for $11. This sheath is designed for attachment to the old-style U.S. Army pistol belt with eyelets, so some users may wish to modify the hanger by

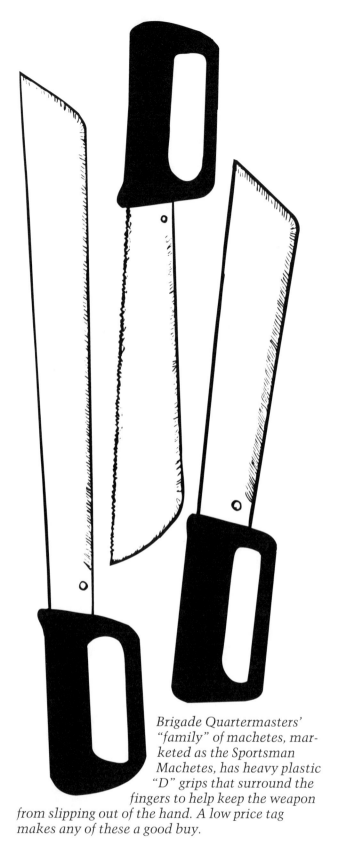

The Modelo Argentino 1909 machete is available from Century International Arms, Inc., and is an excellent buy for those wanting a tough, short-sword-style machete.

Brigade Quartermasters' "family" of machetes, marketed as the Sportsman Machetes, has heavy plastic "D" grips that surround the fingers to help keep the weapon from slipping out of the hand. A low price tag makes any of these a good buy.

adding a cloth, leather, or wire loop so it can be worn on a regular belt. Such a modification is easy to make.

For defensive use, an 18-inch blade seems to be about the maximum length; beyond that there will be problems indoors where low ceilings and narrow hallways make a longer blade awkward (especially given the poor thrusting qualities of the machete design), and the added weight of a longer blade makes the machete unwieldy even if there is room to swing it. That said, blade lengths out to 28 inches are available and, for those seeking such a weapon, Atlanta Cutlery offers one as their Extra Long Machete for just $10.

The Argentine military approached the machete from the sword end of the spectrum with their Modelo Argentino 1909 short sword, made in Germany by Solingen. It has a thicker blade than most machetes and is formed of a higher quality of steel with a large double cross guard and wooden grip plates held in place with rivets. The blade itself swells out near the tip, *bolo* style, and has a sharp point that would accommodate thrusting attacks. With a weight of 1.5 pounds and a blade length of 15.5 inches, the 1909 makes a good weapon for those wanting a defensive blade and is, in fact, still carried by some of Argentina's elite military units.

Sold as surplus, the Modelo Argentino 1909 machete is available for just $25 from Century International Arms, Inc. It is sold in good to very good condition and comes with a sheath. A purchaser will need to remove the heavy

Modern Combat Blades: The Best in Edged Weaponry

Blackjack's Simba (bottom) and Panga (top).

grease the 1909 is packed in and sharpen the edge of the blade, since it generally comes unsharpened. This is not much work and, given the low price tag and quality of the blade, makes it a very good buy.

Given the low prices on the machetes mentioned above and the fact that the thin design of the blade makes for efficient cutting even when made of cheap steels, it's hard to see why anyone would want to shell out more than $30 for a machete and sheath. But a few shoppers always seem to be more concerned with the beauty of a weapon than its utility, and several knife makers have rushed in to capture this market. For most readers, however, the inexpensive machetes mentioned above will give all the power and capabilities of their more expensive brethren, only needing to be sharpened with a file a little more often than blades costing two, three, or even ten times as much. Those who lose or have to abandon a $10 machete won't think twice about the expense; those with an $80 or even $200-plus blade may give it up with a tear in their eye.

Foremost among the "combat machetes" is Al Mar's Pathfinder (mentioned in Chapter 7),

which has a downward slant like the *kukris*, a 14-inch blade, and machete-style handle. The $249 price tag makes this less than ideal for most of those looking for a machete.

Blackjack Knives offers the Panga with a heavy stainless steel 15-inch blade and—unlike a normal machete—a point that allows for thrusting. The grips are Kraton, which aids in holding the blade and acts as a shock absorber to boot. The lack of a swell at the pommel as well as the lack of cross guards make retention and forward thrusts a little iffy, but the quality of Blackjack products and designs is evident with the Panga. The cost is a reasonable $40.

The Blackjack Simba has the grip of the Panga and a 12-inch *bolo*-type blade with a heavy, round edge toward its spear point. Unlike the traditional machete or *bolo*, this one has a sharpened edge down its spine. It weighs 1 pound and costs $75.

• • • • •

In use worldwide, the machete is a tool that is often called upon for defensive needs, usually with devastating results on the user's enemy.

Chapter 9

THE SWORD

Soldiers and fighting experts from Julius Caesar to Richard F. Burton have maintained that an assault with the point of a sword is more effective than a slashing attack. This has been put to the test in actual combat, and the evolution of the sword shows the gradual replacement of wide blades suitable for slashing with narrower, pointed blades. While special conditions sometimes dictated a wider blade (which was the case for those fighting in the confines of a ship's deck, battling opponents encased in armor, or assaulting riders on horseback), the more modern the sword, the more apt it is to be designed for jabbing. Edges are present only for the occasional slash, if at all.

In the early 1900s, both the British and American governments decided to use scientific methods to determine which style of attack was most apt to wound an enemy so they could select new cavalry swords accordingly. While history was to prove that the cavalry attack itself was obsolete with mechanized armies and automatic weapons on the horizon, the research is nevertheless of interest to civilians wondering if a sword might be a practical defensive weapon, especially in areas where ownership of a firearm may be illegal.

The British studies were carried out by the Wilkinson Sword Company; a young George Patton, Jr., was the officer in charge of the American research. Both groups conducted tests of fighters, analyzed fencing theories, and studied battlefield reports of wounds created with bladed weapons during the previous century. After discovering that thrusts were more easily delivered and also more likely to create serious or fatal wounds than cuts, both governments decided to design straight-bladed sabers intended for thrusting rather than slashing attacks. These became the British 1908 trooper saber and the U.S. 1912 cavalry saber.

With automatic weapons able to concentrate huge masses of firepower on an enemy, the modern battlefield has made the sword obsolete. But as noted elsewhere, such firepower is unavailable to citizens, and therefore a bladed weapon is not obsolete for self-defense. Of course, carrying a sword on a dangerous street is not an option for most citizens; a long blade would attract too much attention, and there is just no practical way to conceal such a device. And because canes and umbrellas are rarely carried on a day-to-day basis, hiding one within these utensils is also impractical for all but those who are handicapped—and even then they tend to attract unwanted attention.

But for a homeowner, a long-bladed épée or other sword suitable for stabbing might be a viable self-defense instrument. As mentioned earlier, a person with a knife generally can move fast enough to wound a man holding a gun before the gunman can fire if both are within 15 feet of each other and the man with the blade doesn't telegraph his intentions before commencing his attack. Since many rooms and hallways are less than 15 feet in length, it would seem feasible to mount such a defense. Because a sword has a greater reach than a knife or dagger, it would also seem logical that this would increase the speed of an attack somewhat, giving the swordsman a slight edge.

Furthermore, since the sword has a greater reach, this would enable the swordsman to avoid getting as close to his enemy as would be required with a knife. This minimizes the chances of being hit, grabbed, or shot (depending on what type of counterattack the enemy could mount). Also, with diseases like AIDS being passed between users of intravenous drugs and the high incidence of such drug use among criminals, one might argue that a long-bladed weapon that keeps its user from being splattered with a criminal's blood has an important plus from a health standpoint, too.

Provided the swordsman didn't get his weapon hung up in a low ceiling or telegraph his attack, he would stand a good chance of wounding and even downing an intruder before the man could fire a shot. If the criminal were armed with a knife, crowbar, or similar weapon (as is the case almost 50 percent of the time in the United States), it is likely that the swordsman would have an even greater advantage with a blade capable of reaching over a long distance.

Unlike machetes or Japanese swords with blades longer than 20 inches, which become unwieldy indoors, swords capable of jabbing are practical since the attack is mounted along the open plane between the swordsman and the intruder. Unfortunately, another problem comes into play.

Because jabbing weapons have cutting edges that vary from poor to none, it is possible for an opponent to get "inside" the reach of the blade and be relatively free from danger as he closes and grapples with the swordsman. A quick backward step by the swordsman is the best way to avoid this problem. With luck, the criminal will skewer himself on the blade rather than close on the swordsman. This may not be possible, however, if the swordsman faces multiple opponents or is backed against a wall.

If a foes gets "inside" the point of the blade, then it is necessary to jerk the blade backward or upward so its point is even with the opponent's chest or abdomen and stabbing initiated. This brings the swordsman to the limiting factor on the length of his blade: generally, 35 to 38 inches is the maximum length the average fighter can retract a jab at an opponent who is grappling with him. This is the reason that light swords designed to create stabbing wounds are about this length.

Of course there are other alternatives. One is to have a double edge on the blade. While this wasn't too practical in the past, with modern steels and the serrated edge it's possible to create a lightweight jabbing blade that could leave a savage slash cut if the need arose. (And many traditionally successful short swords like the Roman Gladius are capable of slashing just as effectively as they stab.)

The third alternative would be to carry a second weapon like a dagger in the off hand. An opponent inside the guard would get a jab from the dagger. While this seems like a viable alternative, and it has a historic precedent, the tactic generally was dispensed with as the jabbing sword became lighter. This suggests that a secondary weapon might not be as effective as one might think, especially when facing an opponent armed with a weapon other than a sword.

Because of the mystical reputation of the sword along with the need for tough reproduction swords by reenactment groups and sport

A Roman Gladius like those found at Pompeii.

Celtic Leaf Sword.

fencers, there is a wealth of long-bladed swords in a huge variety of styles available today for anyone wishing to purchase one. Of course, care must be taken not to purchase a "wall hanger" made only for decorative purposes since these normally are poorly tempered and during combat will either take on a figure-eight shape or shatter like glass—either leaving the user all but defenseless.

In addition to wall hangers, it's possible to rule out most medieval swords designed for hacking through armor as well as many pre-1900 cavalry swords designed for slashing foot soldiers from the back of the horse. Ditto for the Middle East's scimitar. This basically leaves two groups to choose from: 1) the short swords and long bayonets (held in the hand rather than mounted on a rifle) and 2) fencing-style swords.

Short swords are for those living in a home or apartment with few wide rooms or halls and/or many corners between doorways. In such an environment, a long sword blade is next to impossible to use and actually will hinder a fighter to the point that he'll look like outtakes from a *Pink Panther* movie. A long-bladed knife or short sword is the weapon of choice in such circumstances.

Long swords are mandated if a fighter will be outdoors or defending a home with wide rooms and long hallways. By carefully planning his defenses, the welder of a jabbing sword can cover such spaces with surprising rapidity, mounting an attack on an opponent even 30 feet away before he can react even if armed with a firearm.

Possibly the most lethal blade in history, the Roman Gladius was a no-nonsense weapon capable of taking out anyone from a spear-wielding barbarian to a noble Greek warrior. The basic design reigned supreme for four centuries as the Romans carved out their empire. Museum Replicas Unlimited offers a Gladius modeled after those found at Pompeii. The replica has a 19.5-inch double-edged blade and a surprisingly comfortable but odd-looking grip. Weighing 2.375 pounds, the blade ends in a sharp point, making it capable of jabs as well as savage chops. It costs $195.

Museum Replicas also offers a similar sword modeled after the Greek sword of 600-500 A.D. (which most historians believe inspired the creation of the Gladius). This sword has a longer 25-inch blade with a weight just under 2 pounds. Like the Gladius, it is capable of both a slashing and stabbing attack. Cost of this replica is $175.

A third lethal short sword design offered by Museum Replicas is the Celtic Leaf Sword. Although the original pattern of this blade goes back to 1300-700 B.C. and was made of bronze, these reproductions are made from steel. With more than a passing resemblance to the Roman Gladius, the Celtic sword has slightly better chopping power thanks to its curved edge, and its point penetrates better, too. The blade is 19.25 inches long and the weight is 26 ounces. Cost is $170.

Some of the best buys available for those searching for a short sword are offered in the form of "sword" bayonets manufactured during the late 1800s and early 1900s when firearms were displacing swords and bayonets on the battlefield. Many of these are made of excellent steels, are suitable for jabbing attacks, and have thin blades that can take a single edge for slashing attacks, too.

Century International Arms, Inc., has an excellent assortment of such blades, including many bayonets having 15-inch or longer blades. Among the best of these are the Argentine 1909 Sabre bayonet with wooden grips, a weight of only 1 pound, and a 15.5-inch blade (and a low price tag of just $18); the similar 1891 Mauser bayonet with chrome or metal grips, a 1.25-pound weight, and a 15.5-inch blade (costing only $18); and the Brazilian M1908/34 bayonet, originally made in Ger-

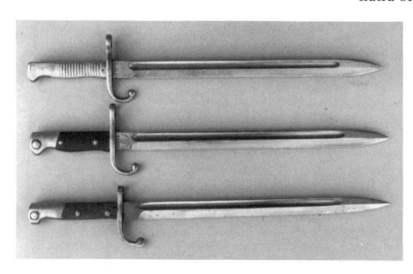

Three "sword bayonets" currently offered on the surplus market by Century International Arms, Inc.

many with a 1.25-pound weight and a 15-inch blade ($20).

All three of these surplus bayonets are sold by Century Arms in good to very good condition and come with sheaths. Purchasers will need to remove the heavy grease they are stored in and sharpen the edge of the blades since they generally come in an unsharpened condition. This is not much work and, given

For those desiring a long sword for defense of a home, the rapier is ideal due to its length and light weight.

their low price tag and high quality, makes them very good buys.

For those desiring a long sword, the ideal choice is the rapier. Museum Replicas Limited offers "modular" reproduction rapier blades with hilt/cross guard and grip assemblies. Since most of those needing a self-defense weapon at home have no need for the cross guard on a rapier (it was designed to protect the hand of the user from an opponent's sword), purchasing only the blade and grip and improvising spacers to "take up the slack" where the cross guard would normally be can result in a huge savings. (And even more money can be saved by those who create a grip assembly in their home shop.)

Museum Replicas' blades are priced at $40 for the 36-inch, 6-ounce Musketeer, or $120 for the 38-inch, 10.5-ounce Rapier (which is probably best left to tall users due to its long length; recovering from an opponent inside one's guard would be difficult for a shorter user). Grips to go on these blades cost $16 (with a choice of brass or twisted steel wire wrap). A simple brass cross guard and swept-line hilt costs an additional $80, and a steel-cup hilt assembly costs $60.

Museum Replicas also sells the assembled rapiers in the form of their Swept Hilt Rapier weighing 2.75 pounds with a 38-inch blade and a cost of $269, and a Cup Hilt Rapier, which has a similar blade length, a weight of 2.125 pounds, and a cost of $249. Scabbards are available for these at an additional $62.

As mentioned in Chapter 5, those living near a university with a fencing program often can purchase a scarred and rusty épée or foil for very little. Simply grinding the "button" end of the blade into a point will transform a

Those living near a university with a fencing program often can locate an épée or foil that can be purchased for a song. With a point ground onto it, this would make a viable weapon.

sporter into a real fighting tool at a bargain-basement price.

Whether using a rusty survivor of a college athletic program or a reproduction of the Roman Gladius, great thought must be given to mounting an attack, studying the problem realistically with the head rather than the heart (and forgetting all the romantic sword duels seen in the movies). Practice is essential with any bladed weapon and especially so with

a sword if the user is to learn how to wield it as a modern combat blade.

The nearest public library will likely have several good books on fencing. All that's really needed for a modern swordsman who won't likely be facing a similarly armed opponent is the ability to mount quick lunging attacks and recover rapidly afterward, perhaps also learning to block any counterattack an opponent might attempt. Unfortunately, many books are long on theory and contain umpteen ways of attacking, yet all that's needed is one good one since fights in real life will be over in seconds. And many books on sword fighting ignore or refuse to see the shortcomings of the fighting style they espouse (this is especially true of Oriental fighting techniques, which are, when it comes to sword fighting, generally inferior to Western styles).

One good book that gives a tough, *realistic*, and somewhat unorthodox look at both Oriental and Western styles of swordsmanship is Marc "Animal" MacYoung's *Pool Cues, Beer Bottles, and Baseball Bats*. As MacYoung points out in his book, many of the techniques used in wielding a sword can be adapted to pool cues, sticks, canes, or other "environmental" objects that might be at a user's disposal when he's away from home—and his sword.

Chapter 10

BATTLE-AXES, MEAT CLEAVERS, AND FOLDING SHOVELS

A s with swords and dagger designs, one good way to judge the effectiveness of a weapon is to see how it's done when used in actual combat on a regular basis. The Romans apparently never used axes in combat, while the enemies they faced used both small and large battle-axes. Axes apparently were common in Mycenaean and Cretan armies, too. Notably, all those using the ax were on the losing side.

Axes started to be seen on European battlefields in the 1500s, but often as secondary weapons/tools such as those carried by archers. Knights often carried a war hammer (similar to modern hammers but with a spike rather than claws behind the head), and the poleax became useful for foot soldiers needing to attack horsemen. But these were specialized weapons and, in the case of poleaxes, too big and awkward for use by modern fighters.

So for the most part, battle-axes competing against swords and other weapons have come up second best; consequently, they were replaced on the battlefield by the sword, spear, and bows and arrows of various types. The reason for this becomes obvious when one studies the techniques needed to wield an ax—its weight makes the first blow crucial since, if it fails to connect, the wielder is left off balance and will be hard-pressed to recover and deliver a second strike before the enemy can initiate an attack of his own.

Furthermore, unlike a sword or large knife, the blade of an ax is small compared to the length of its handle. If the blade connects, it creates a devastating wound, but if it misses, it creates only a large welt or—with luck—a fractured bone. Like a miss, however, this half-effective blow will likely allow a foe to return the favor, probably more effectively. And the length of the handle leaves a large area where an opponent might obtain a hold, tying up the weapon while a counterattack is launched.

On the other hand, nothing inspires fear like an ax. Just as the sight of a Viking with his battle-ax inspired many a European to surrender without a fight, the thought of being struck with an ax could put a criminal to flight. But this psychological edge is not as great as one might hope, especially if facing a criminal flying high on drugs. So realism, not hope or fantasy, must be the guiding power when a fighter decides whether or not an ax is suitable for his purposes.

There is little doubt that the ax—or similar bladed weapons like the meat cleaver or even the sharpened shovel—can be effective under certain conditions. In times when an opponent may be too close to use a firearm (for fear of hitting a comrade) or when both are armed with bladed weapons, an ax may have the proverbial edge (pun intended) on a less substantial weapon like a short-bladed knife. Then the brutal power of the ax—which can slash through a light barrier or even a wall and disable a foe, even with a "minor" hit to a limb—may win the day. But courage and skill are called for with such weapons, and probably more than a smattering of luck. (In fact, it appears that the folding shovel issued to GIs in Vietnam killed more Vietcong than the bayonet on the end of a rifle ever came close to doing.)

In addition to the slow recovery time and small edge on the ax and similar weapons, the effectiveness of these fighting tools because of their size and weight has another downside; they are too heavy to be carried easily for any length of time and nearly impossible to conceal. These facts alone make the ax and its cousins unsuitable for many people interested in edged weapons.

Furthermore, many of the effective ancient versions of these weapons are just too massive for anyone in their right mind to use. Today's fighters had best forget full-size battle-axes and halberds since they're too heavy to carry and too immense for indoor combat, which is precisely where many citizens will need an edged weapon. With most attacks initiated with an overhead stroke, a modern combat ax must have a relatively short overall length (of 2 feet or less) if it is being used indoors in most modern buildings.

Fortunately, there are short, lightweight versions of the ax that might be useful as weapons. Like the machete, many of these have the added plus of being useful as woodworking or other tools, providing them the "respectability" of a tool pressed into service

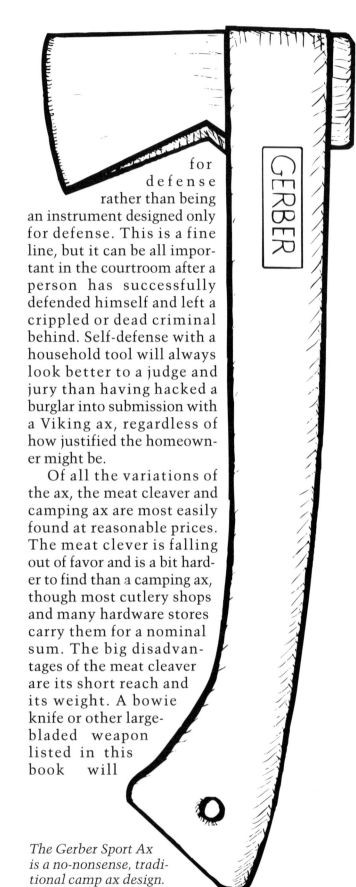

for defense rather than being an instrument designed only for defense. This is a fine line, but it can be all important in the courtroom after a person has successfully defended himself and left a crippled or dead criminal behind. Self-defense with a household tool will always look better to a judge and jury than having hacked a burglar into submission with a Viking ax, regardless of how justified the homeowner might be.

Of all the variations of the ax, the meat cleaver and camping ax are most easily found at reasonable prices. The meat clever is falling out of favor and is a bit harder to find than a camping ax, though most cutlery shops and many hardware stores carry them for a nominal sum. The big disadvantages of the meat cleaver are its short reach and its weight. A bowie knife or other large-bladed weapon listed in this book will

The Gerber Sport Ax is a no-nonsense, traditional camp ax design.

Modern Combat Blades: The Best in Edged Weaponry

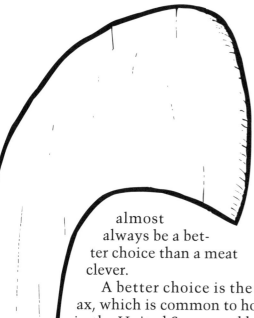

The futuristic Dozier Ax is just as capable of combat as other more conventional axes.

almost always be a better choice than a meat clever.

A better choice is the camping ax, which is common to households in the United States and has been a comfort to many, both during home break-ins as well as when a bear is sniffing around a campsite. A variety of such blades is available at reasonable prices at most hardware and discount stores, often for less than $10 to $20. (Larger axes are also available but generally will be unsuitable for combat due to length and weight.)

For those wanting a bit more quality, most of the knife manufacturers offer high-end axes suitable for camping or defensive use. Gerber offers a Sport Ax for $54. It is 14 inches long and weighs 21.3 ounces. Blackjack carries a stylized Viking Raider Axe with a Kraton handle and a $120 price tag. A.G. Russell's custom-made, futuristic Dozier Ax weighs 25 ounces, has an overall length of 11.5 inches, and costs $275. B&T Tools offers the Bush-Wakkers with a 5- and 7-inch blade. The heads can be removed from the factory handle for remounting on a grip of the owner's choice, giving a custom fit for those wishing to go to some extra effort.

A short shovel or, for those outdoors, even a full-size shovel can also be used as a brutal weapon. The key to making these more effec-

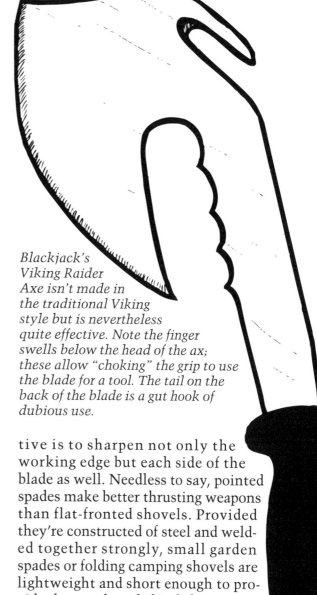

Blackjack's Viking Raider Axe isn't made in the traditional Viking style but is nevertheless quite effective. Note the finger swells below the head of the ax; these allow "choking" the grip to use the blade for a tool. The tail on the back of the blade is a gut hook of dubious use.

tive is to sharpen not only the working edge but each side of the blade as well. Needless to say, pointed spades make better thrusting weapons than flat-fronted shovels. Provided they're constructed of steel and welded together strongly, small garden spades or folding camping shovels are lightweight and short enough to provide the speed needed in fighting.

Like the ax, shovels have a genuine validity and will never be legislated out of existence. Thus they will "look good" if the user finds himself in a court of law after maiming a criminal who had been intent on doing injury and instead became the victim of an angry homeowner. One of the few books that studies fighting with shovels—and any number of common tools and weapons—is Marc "Animal" MacYoung's *Pool Cues, Beer Bottles, and Baseball Bats*, available from Paladin Press. Many of the fighting techniques listed in his book could also be adapted to the ax.

A tool created in the early 1800s for

American pioneers that was adopted in the late 1800s by the Chinese and has recently been revived and imported into America lends itself to combat use. Sold as the Frontiersman's Tool or Multi-Purpose Hatchet, this versatile tool has a hatchet on one side of its head and a hammer on the opposite face. A pry bar extends from its top and a nail puller is located partway down its handle. Best of all, it has a solid metal handle with two grip plates on either side. This makes for a very tough tool with a price tag of less than $10 to $20 and a weight of 2 pounds. It can be found in many hardware stores or ordered from U.S. Cavalry for $8.

Pioneers crossing the West with their multipurpose tools often came face-to-face with Indians armed with tomahawks. Though American Indians often carried these weapons, their indigenous weapons were throwing sticks. The techniques of using the sticks were adapted to the small steel axes imported from Europe by traders. In fact, the tomahawks that settlers often faced in combat were actually steel axes that had been sold to the Indians by white traders; this is the reason the tomahawk so closely resembles the European steel ax. (The word "tomahawk" is the anglicized Algonquin Indian word given to the small ax.)

The tomahawk is a versatile weapon that is also useful for chopping, clubbing, or throwing at game animals. Its light weight makes for fast recovery from missed strokes, doing away with some of the shortcomings of a battle-ax. This made it an ideal tool for the nomadic American Indian, and more than a few European immigrants undoubtedly carried similar axes for the same reason. The tomahawk was employed as a weapon on both sides during the French and Indian War and was "standard issue" with Rogers' Rangers (led by Robert Rogers), viewed by many as the first "unconventional combat" force in the world. American troops carried the tomahawk in the Revolutionary War and during the War of 1812.

A few American troops carried tomahawks in World War II (apparently Nazi soldiers were terrified of the weapon, and Hitler's propaganda machine often publicized its use by GIs as a sign of U.S. barbarism). The tomahawk was later wielded by a handful of Americans battling against the Vietcong under the encouragement of Peter La Gana, who tried to incorporate the weapon into the U.S. Army's equipment.

Although Hollywood and contests have made most people view the tomahawk as a weapon that is only thrown, in fact it can be and often was hand-held for combat and undoubtedly worked just as effectively as the other axes listed in this chapter. Furthermore, it must be noted that throwing a bladed weapon often isn't wise in practice because of the damage it does to the weapon as well as the fact that it leaves the user defenseless if he doesn't have a secondary weapon and gives the enemy a weapon if there is a miss. Additionally, like most other thrown weapons, the tomahawk is usually effective only if thrown at a known range.

For those wishing to throw a tomahawk, the best ones designed for this purpose have a hickory stock (or a metal tang in the case of modern axes) and a deep "eye" in the hatchet head so the grip won't break with a bad throw. For best results, the tomahawk should have the upper edge of its head swept up at least an inch above the rest of the surface at the top of the shaft. This upper corner is known as the "leading edge" by tomahawk throwers; it almost always connects with the target first.

For accuracy, the best overall length generally is agreed to be around 16 inches from the base of the handle to the top of the head. One trick for improving accuracy during a throw is to place the thumb over the grip so it "points" in the direction the tomahawk should go when released.

With the recent interest in black powder weapons, mountain men, and eighteenth and nineteenth century ways of doing things, more than a few areas have knife and tomahawk throwing contests. This has created a market for inexpensive tomahawks, and Atlanta Cutlery has gone after the market with its Competition Tomahawk. It weighs 22 ounces and costs $15.

A modern modification of the tomahawk design is the double-bladed Tru-Throw Hatchet from Brigade Quartermasters. This weapon has a second double blade on its head so it can be thrown with either side facing forward. This makes it quicker to bring into action and also increases the chance of a serious wound if the thrower's aim is off. The $25 Tru-Throw has a short 8.5-inch length and weighs only a pound, making it easy to carry. (Do-it-yourselfers can increase the likelihood of a serious injury to an enemy with the Tru-Throw by removing the scale grips and grinding a point onto the base of the grip. This will guarantee a serious injury

The West African hunga-munga has multiple blades that increase the likelihood of creating maximum damage when the weapon connects with the target.

even if the grip rather than the head of the ax strikes first.)

While the tomahawk was becoming popular in the Americas, the West Africans were perfecting the *hunga-munga*, which, unlike throwing knives and tomahawks, could connect with a target at a variety of ranges and do damage thanks to a multitude of sharp edges and points on its head and grip. Thrown with the blades horizontal, the *hunga-munga* is capable of severing limbs at 20 yards.

Atlanta Cutlery carries a copy of the *hunga-munga*, made in India by the same contractors that make military *kukris*. The big plus of the Atlanta Cutlery version of this African ax is that the steel blade is left relatively soft so throwing can't fracture it and, if the blade is bent during practice, it can be straightened out. Cost of the 1.5-pound weapon is $40.

Whether throwing a tomahawk or a *hunga-munga*, those using these blades for self-defense must remember that once thrown, the blade is gone. Therefore, it is essential to have a secondary weapon for backup if there are multiple opponents or the ax fails to fully incapacitate an enemy.

For those not needing a throwing ax, reproductions of smaller ancient battle-axes are available. Those selecting such axes for self-defense may wish to create a "collection" of ancient weapons to help justify their ownership of the blade to local authorities.

One of these reproductions is the Ren-

Brigade Quartermasters' Tru-Throw (left), shown here next to a well-used antique camping ax.

Battle-Axes, Meat Cleavers, and Folding Shovels

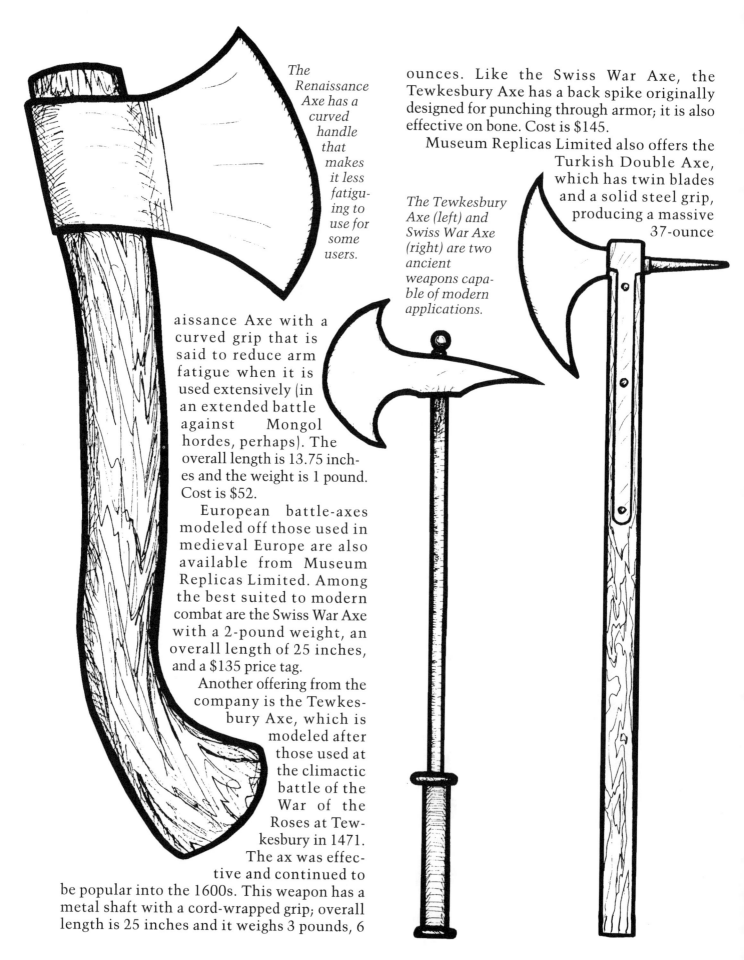

The Renaissance Axe has a curved handle that makes it less fatiguing to use for some users.

ounces. Like the Swiss War Axe, the Tewkesbury Axe has a back spike originally designed for punching through armor; it is also effective on bone. Cost is $145.

Museum Replicas Limited also offers the Turkish Double Axe, which has twin blades and a solid steel grip, producing a massive 37-ounce

The Tewkesbury Axe (left) and Swiss War Axe (right) are two ancient weapons capable of modern applications.

aissance Axe with a curved grip that is said to reduce arm fatigue when it is used extensively (in an extended battle against Mongol hordes, perhaps). The overall length is 13.75 inches and the weight is 1 pound. Cost is $52.

European battle-axes modeled off those used in medieval Europe are also available from Museum Replicas Limited. Among the best suited to modern combat are the Swiss War Axe with a 2-pound weight, an overall length of 25 inches, and a $135 price tag.

Another offering from the company is the Tewkesbury Axe, which is modeled after those used at the climactic battle of the War of the Roses at Tewkesbury in 1471. The ax was effective and continued to be popular into the 1600s. This weapon has a metal shaft with a cord-wrapped grip; overall length is 25 inches and it weighs 3 pounds, 6

Modern Combat Blades: The Best in Edged Weaponry

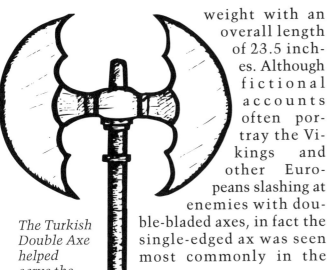

weight with an overall length of 23.5 inches. Although fictional accounts often portray the Vikings and other Europeans slashing at enemies with double-bladed axes, in fact the single-edged ax was seen most commonly in the West. But in the Middle East, the double blade ruled, helping carve out the Turkish empire from 1450 to 1850 A.D. It worked then and it will work today as an effective ax for those looking for a combat blade. The price tag for this modern version is $135.

• • • • •

Whether using a replica of an ancient weapon or a modern camping version from the corner hardware store, the ax is a fearsome weapon that demands skill and cunning in its use since its weight and configuration often limit its user to one massive blow when facing an opponent.

The Turkish Double Axe helped carve the Turkish Empire and is capable of "whittling down" today's criminal element.

Chapter 11
THROWING BLADES

*I*n addition to the tomahawk and *hunga-munga*, there are any number of knifelike blades that can be tossed at an enemy. Before going further, there are several key points that must again be stressed.

One is that throwing a primary weapon at an enemy is a poor tactic that's likely to get the person trying it killed. Therefore, thrown blades should be secondary weapons, with the primary weapon held in reserve.

Secondly, a thrown blade is unlikely to down or kill an opponent. Those who hunt deer or wild pigs with throwing knives are quick to admit that animals are rarely killed with a single strike of a knife. A second or third knife must be thrown at the prey, and often a separate coup de grace administered upon closing with a wounded animal. Unless the fighter is willing to pin his hopes on pure luck, he should view thrown blades as harassing, distracting, or maiming tools rather than primary weapons.

Unlike an arrow or spear, a throwing knife tumbles in flight. This means its point only connects with a target at intervals when its tip is oriented toward the target. If the thrower releases his blade at the wrong instant (which is likely if an enemy is charging or otherwise moving), the blade will strike with its butt or side, doing little damage and perhaps even spurring the enemy to faster action before a second blade can be thrown. Knife throwers can become good at judging distances, and homeowners can pace off distances in a house to enable them to throw a knife when a criminal "crosses the line." But anyone planning on doing this has greatly limited his options and left little room for the unexpected (thereby ignoring the caveat that the unexpected should be anticipated in combat).

Because of the jarring impact a blade receives when colliding with a target, the blade of a throwing knife must not be tempered to the extent of most other combat knives. If it is, it will snap off or crack with use (and throwing a standard knife is a quick way to destroy it).

The first quality throwing knives available in the United States were from

Randall Knives and the Tru-Balance Knife Company. Both created excellent designs executed in quality materials. Many other companies have since followed the lead of Randall and Tru-Balance, so a wide range of sizes and prices is available today in the way of throwing knives.

For combat, a heavy knife is called for, preferably with one edge sharpened to maximize the cutting of arteries and nerves as the point penetrates an opponent. The heavy weight is essential in order for the blade to gain enough energy to penetrate adequately; lightweight blades of less than a pound and a half are likely to create only superficial wounds unless they chance to strike an eye.

Most throwing knives have large blades with minimal grips (and a few even have the end of the grip sharpened to facilitate wounding even if the weapon hits handle first). For best results, the overall length should be 11 to 16 inches, with the balance point at the center or perhaps an inch behind the center.

There are any number of ways to throw a knife. Those who throw it by holding the grip generally have best results if the blade is released with a vertical orientation; those throwing by holding the blade release it with its flat plane in a horizontal orientation. Grip-thrown knives can have both of their edges sharpened for added capabilities. Blade-held throwing knives should have only one sharpened edge, with the other edge held toward the palm during the throw to avoid cutting the hand upon release. Most experts agree that a graceful follow-through, similar to that used by a baseball pitcher, is essential to obtain both the velocity and accuracy desired in throwing knives, and that during the throw the wrist must not be snapped but kept rigid.

A knife thrower should experiment until he finds the correct "ranges" that allow the point

Throwing knives come in a bewildering number of shapes and sizes but generally have a double blade that's wider and heavier than that of hand-held combat knives. Many have minimal grips—often simply paint on the tang—and sometimes the tang is pointed to create a wound even if the knife strikes with the wrong orientation.

Modern Combat Blades: The Best in Edged Weaponry

The ballistic knife can be used as a standard dagger or, with the arming pin removed, fired by means of the cross-guard-like trigger.

of the knife to connect with the target. These generally will be at yard intervals of 5, 8, 11, 14, etc., with 2 yards taken in the throw and 3 for each spin of the blade—though this will vary with the blade and thrower. Once the spacing is determined, the thrower should then carefully measure the distances at which the point hits and always work at one of these distances when honing his skills. He should also take the time to develop the ability to estimate these distances or pace them off in the area that will be defended, using furniture or other reference points for orientation.

The best source of throwing knives is Gutmann, which carries everything from quality German-made hunting-style throwing knives to inexpensive Japanese versions. Among the best suited for combat throwing are the Professional with a 13-inch overall length and the 11-inch Black Mamba. U.S. Cavalry also carries a pair of useful throwing knives, the 10-inch Thrower III for $25 and the 10.5-inch Blazing Arrow II for $13, either of which would make a good combat thrower.

Whichever style a purchaser goes with, it is wise to buy at least three identical knives so skills can be honed and, if the sparks begin to fly, three throws, rather than one, can be made at an enemy. When practicing, it is wise to use as many different targets as there are knives to avoid having them hit and damage each other during practice.

If the blade of the throwing knife could be kept from tumbling, then the thrower's task would be greatly simplified. At least three systems have been created that do this. The simplest was created by the Chinese; it consists of a handkerchief-sized cloth tied to the tail of the grip. This keeps the point of the blade forward as it travels toward the target. The catch is that the blade takes a short distance to orient itself and the cloth acts like a parachute, quickly dropping the speed of the projectile. Nonetheless, this may be a solution for those throwing at medium ranges, and some readers may wish to experiment with it.

Another system is to modify the knife design so it is transformed into a dart, somewhat like a short arrow with nearly all of its weight forward on the blade and the minuscule grip finned to force the point to remain forward. This, too, takes a short distance to become stabilized after being thrown but doesn't experience much of a velocity drop once this occurs (especially when compared to the cloth-stabilized blade).

The third system is the "ballistic knife," which is launched by a heavy spring rather than being thrown. While this system would seem to be ideal, getting the blade crammed into its launcher over a heavy spring is hairy, and accidental launching becomes a real concern, dictating an arming pin similar to that on a hand grenade. This makes the weapon rather slow to launch.

The ballistic knife is believed to have been developed by the Soviets for their special forces. The Spye Knife Company marketed American-made copies in the United States during the mid-1980s. As with all other types of guns, knives, cars, baseball bats, and the like, the ballistic knife was sometimes seen in the hands of criminals. (On occasions when law enforcement personnel confiscated the weapon, they sometimes fired it accidentally while inspecting it. State police bulletins were issued warning officers not to fool with the devices if they impounded them.)

The U.S. Congress soon was conducting hearings on the ballistic knife, which, if one was to believe the testimonies given, was on the verge of falling into the hands of every petty criminal in the country. Demonstrations of the knife ("firing accurately out to 30 feet!") were given, complete with the penetration of lightweight ballistic vests (which could also be penetrated by conventional daggers and thin-bladed knives, a fact omitted in testimony). In 1989, Congress banned civilian ownership of the ballistic knife.

Since the American-made version of the knife had been popular, the Spye Knife Company began selling two legal versions of

Perhaps the best-known of these is the *shuriken*, or Japanese throwing star. While the ability to throw these accurately demands skill, they have the added plus of being able to connect with one of many points.

Styles of traditional throwing stars vary from three or four points to as many eight, all of which have sharpened edges to promote penetration. They can be thrown in at least three different ways: backhand, overhand, or from the side. Considerable practice is needed to attain the ability to hit accurately and create a serious wound.

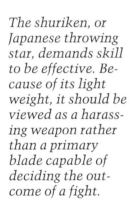

The shuriken, or Japanese throwing star, demands skill to be effective. Because of its light weight, it should be viewed as a harassing weapon rather than a primary blade capable of deciding the outcome of a fight.

the blade-launching system. One was simply the knife and launcher without its spring; the other was the launcher and spring (both sized so they wouldn't fit the knife version) with a solid metal baton or grappling hook replacing the blade. Both carried a price tag in the vicinity of $85. While it doesn't take much skill to modify either of these legal versions of the ballistic knife system, the effort is of dubious value given the illegality of the conversion and the slowness, limited range, and one-shot abilities of the blade.

Just as the *hunga-munga* improved on the idea of the tomahawk by adding more cutting edges to its design so blade orientation and range were less of a consideration when throwing, multibladed knives and similar instruments have been created to improve the chances of damaging a foe when the device is thrown.

The standard *shuriken* isn't as effective as one might hope, however, due to its light weight, dictated by the fact that the original weapon was designed to be carried hidden on the person. An additional mark against the throwing star is the fact that many municipalities have banned it (due to its popularity with teens who OD'd on kung-fu movies). But for those wanting a *shuriken* for harassing an enemy, traditional patterns are available from Catoctin Cutlery and Brigade Quartermasters Ltd.

Do-it-yourselfers may wish to create their own *shurikens* from sheet metal or an old circular saw blade (which even has the traditional center hole that allows *shuriken* to be held together on a string when carried). By increasing its weight and size, a throwing star can take on some real authority.

The Japanese created similar types of throwing blades with points in three dimensions in a spherical pattern as opposed to the flat configuration of the throwing star. These are known as the *arare* (spiked ball) and *tetsubishi* (similar to the European caltrops).

The *arare* is thrown much like a ball, while the *tetsubishi* is most often dropped when its owner is being pursued. It lands with one of its spikes pointing up, ready to slash the foot of the pursuer. Catoctin Cutlery offers *tetsubishi* as its Ninja Caltrops. In addition to being dangerous to those on foot, they will also puncture vehicle tires, making them sort of the land mine of the blade world.

Bo Randall and other knife makers have also experimented with multibladed throwing knives that have come to be known in the West as "spinners." With their longer blades and heavier weight, these are more effective than the throwing star.

Many spinners are easier to carry than throwing stars, being designed so their blades pivot around a common point, allowing them to be folded and carried in a belt sheath. Once drawn, the spinner can be quickly unfolded, the blades locked, and the device thrown with a flick of the wrist, creating a lethal spinning weapon. Like the other weapons listed in this chapter, spinners are "one-shot" devices, so those using them should have several as well as a hand-held weapon to fall back on.

Like the throwing star, spinners are easily fabricated from sheet metal. A central hole and bolt (secured with a quick-tightening wing nut) can even be used to create a folding spinner. Pointed, daggerlike blades are ideal, and at

least one cutting edge will enhance the blades' abilities.

For those wishing to purchase a spinner, Catoctin Cutlery has three models, including the four-bladed Star-Knife (costing $4.25), a six-bladed Star-Knife ($4.75), and a Throwing Cross, with greater mass and a

Spinners are designed so their blades pivot around a common point, allowing them to be folded and carried in a belt sheath.

knifelike grip (users should grind the grip to a point to improve its chances of wounding an opponent), for $6.75.

• • • • •

Thrown blades are not for everyone. If used, they should be considered only as harassing, secondary weapons that buy the knife thrower time or take the fight out of an attacker. They are not always effective and seldom quick in stopping an opponent.

Chapter 12

EVERYTHING ELSE

Because a cutting blade is found on many tools, there is an endless number of instruments that can be pressed into service as weapons. Among the better of these are straight razors, utility knives, flooring tools, and so on. But most of these aren't as effective as standard knives and—if carried on the street—are apt to be treated as concealed weapons even in areas where 4-inch folding knives can be carried. So the idea that a common household object carried on the street is legally safer than a knife is not always true. And given the fact that such tools are less-effective fighting implements, anybody carrying one places himself in double jeopardy.

Of the items mentioned above, the straight razor is the one seen most commonly on the streets. Although a razor will create some ugly cuts and generally has a high "fear factor" among those facing it, it is not overly effective since it produces wounds only through slashing. A razor can be deadly with an attack to the throat, but this is a hard target to reach, especially if the opponent is aware of an attack being mounted.

Razor blades were exempted from the federal switchblade laws passed by Congress. Though they were not specifically exempted in the bill itself, they can legally be of a design that makes them capable of being opened quickly with one hand. As with other blades, however, a straight razor carried in the pocket may be considered a concealed weapon if it isn't apparent that the user has a legitimate reason to have it (and needing to shave while walking a city street is a dubious argument at best). Razor blades are readily available at most drugstores and can be ordered from most cutlery companies, but they should be considered second choice to many other bladed weapons.

Because cutting blades and daggers are easily fabricated from metal or removed from kitchen knives or folders and epoxied into common items like lipstick tubes, cigarette lighters, toes of shoes, and so forth, concealable weapons created from such items abound. Also, simple expedients like placing an unsheathed dagger inside a paper sack or a short sword inside a box make it possible to camouflage almost any combat knife. So there is an endless array of concealable or concealed blades that a person can create or encounter.

Among the more common hidden blades sold commercially are those designed to look like belt buckles. The belt buckle knife is not without its shortcomings, however. Those needing a belt to hold up their pants may find themselves at a distinct disadvantage if it is necessary to release the belt in order to remove the bladed buckle. One solution to this problem is to create a separate knife that comes out of the buckle, leaving the belt in place.

With a few quick motions, this Bowen belt buckle is transformed into a push dagger. (Photo courtesy of Atlanta Cutlery)

Good examples of this solution are seen in the Sportman's Buckle offered by Gutmann and the Executive belt buckle by Al Mar. These stainless steel folders come with buckles that

Al Mar's Executive combines a small folder with a belt buckle. (Drawing courtesy of Al Mar)

fit a belt with a width of 1.5 inch or less. The small folder slides out of the buckle into the grasping hand, though the blade then needs to be unfolded, making this system slow to get into play.

A second problem with the hidden dagger belt buckle design is that the blade length is limited by the curvature of the waistband. Consequently, most belt buckle knives are very short and often of a push dagger design, with the buckle portion acting as the grip of the blade.

Among the best-known belt buckle knives are the Bowen Knife Company's designs available from Atlanta Cutlery. These come in three models: the Model 209 with a single-edged 2.875-inch blade, the Model 205 with a dagger-style 2.875-inch blade, and the Model 202 with

a 2.5-inch single-edged blade (designed for narrower belts). All are made of stainless steel and cost from $23 to $27. These knives are easily recognizable since they don't have a buckle tongue, and in states like California, where they are considered to be concealed weapons, policemen have been quick to spot them and arrest the wearer.

U.S. Cavalry offers a similar dagger-style knife with a 2-inch brass dagger. This belt buckle knife is very ornate and comes with a brown leather belt. Cost is $25.

Tekna offered its Credit Card knife that is the size of its namesake (though thicker), and the now-defunct The Edge Company copied this as its Security Card. These had wide blades that could be shoved out by pushing on a button running down the middle of the "card." Due to the poor grip offered by the flat body of these knives, they were not overly popular.

What has become known as The Executive Edge is another popular concealed blade that appears to be an ink pen when hanging in a shirt pocket. In fact it is a narrow-bladed knife. Marketed by B&D Trading Company, The Executive Edge lacks locking features, and the time needed to unfold the 2-inch blade makes it less than ideal as a defensive weapon.

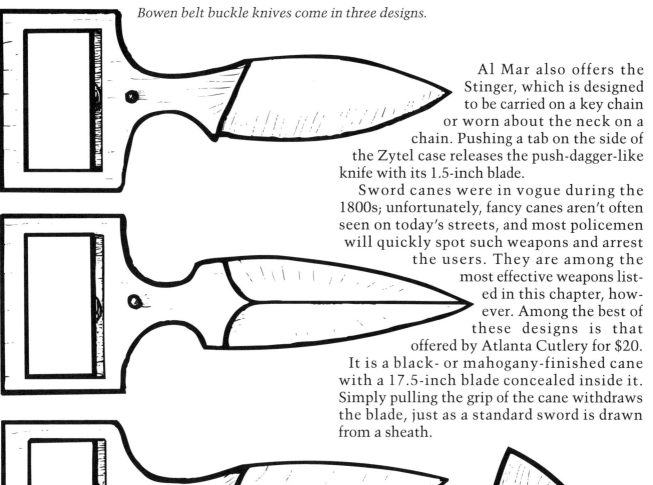

Bowen belt buckle knives come in three designs.

Al Mar also offers the Stinger, which is designed to be carried on a key chain or worn about the neck on a chain. Pushing a tab on the side of the Zytel case releases the push-dagger-like knife with its 1.5-inch blade.

Sword canes were in vogue during the 1800s; unfortunately, fancy canes aren't often seen on today's streets, and most policemen will quickly spot such weapons and arrest the users. They are among the most effective weapons listed in this chapter, however. Among the best of these designs is that offered by Atlanta Cutlery for $20. It is a black- or mahogany-finished cane with a 17.5-inch blade concealed inside it. Simply pulling the grip of the cane withdraws the blade, just as a standard sword is drawn from a sheath.

Metal "pens" with spring-loaded ice-pick-style blades have also been marketed. These are often quick to bring into play but have many of the disadvantages of ice picks, and their 3-inch blades generally make them less than ideal for combat. This design was first seen in the OSS's Lancet and has been marketed in the United States as the Guardfather and Inner City Sportsman's Pencil.

One quick-to-bring-into-play concealed knife is Al Mar's Wild Hair, which appears to be a stainless steel comb when carried in the pocket. When the "comb" is removed, it proves to have a 3-inch dagger on its end. It costs $25. (Other variations on this design are seen with plastic combs mated to metal blades, or even Zytel combs with sharpened plastic blades on their tail ends.)

Another effective weapon is Brigade Quartermasters' All-Protection Sword Umbrella, which, in addition to working as a quality umbrella, conceals a 10-inch ice-pick-style blade. This is less

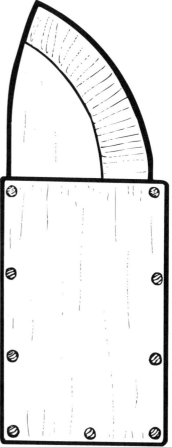

The Security Card is a thick plastic case that conceals a wide, retractable blade.

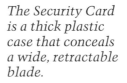

Al Mar's Wild Hair appears to be a stainless steel comb when carried in the pocket, but is actually a 3-inch dagger. (Drawing courtesy of Al Mar)

apt to be spotted by law enforcement personnel but also is out of place on any other day than a rainy one. Cost is $50.

Those wanting to look at the many other concealed bladed weapons that have been created should see Mark Smith's *Hidden Threat*, available from Paladin Press.

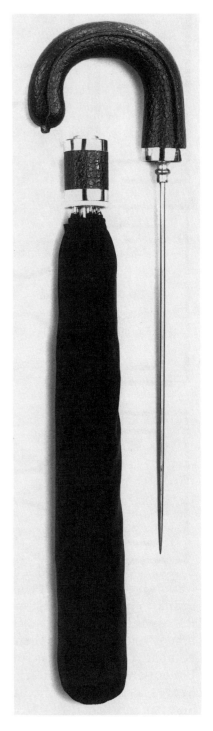

Brigade Quartermasters' All-Protection Sword Umbrella conceals a 10-inch ice-pick-style blade. (Photo courtesy of Brigade Quartermasters)

Modern Combat Blades: The Best in Edged Weaponry

Chapter 13
TOMORROW'S COMBAT BLADES

*J*ust as modern materials have changed the makeup, weight, and designs of everything from cars and jets to peanut butter jars and firearms, so new materials are changing the makeup of combat blades. In fact, today's hobbyist knifesmiths are creating knives of a quality that their forefathers only dreamed of. Companies like Atlanta Cutlery and Jantz Supply offer blade blanks and nearly finished blades that require only a little shaping, polishing, and sharpening coupled with a waterproof micarta or similar handle to create an excellent combat blade for a minimum amount of money. (For a closer look at the many techniques that can be used to create a combat blade—even from scratch—see Jim Hrisoulas' excellent volumes, *The Complete Bladesmith* and *The Master Bladesmith*, which demonstrate the techniques needed to create beautiful, quality custom blades.)

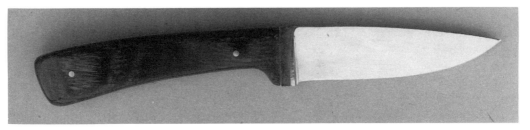

Today's hobbyist knifesmiths are creating knives of a quality that their forefathers only dreamed of. Shown here is one such blade, with micarta grips and a stainless steel blade, created by George Guillory.

No one can reliably predict where the availability of new materials will lead knife designers. Yet already, ceramic blades that almost never need to be sharpened are showing up on kitchen knives; presently these are too brittle for combat, but this may change in the near future. And plastic daggers like those created by Choate Machine & Tool demonstrate that light, strong, nonmetal

Tomorrow's combat blades will be thinner and sharper thanks to stronger alloys and materials. Points and edges that would be too weak to construct with today's materials will likely create superior—and durable—cutting and stabbing blades in the near future.

combat blades are not only possible but practical.

Today, expensive custom knives with titanium and steel melded together with complex dovetails or folds are found at knife shows. One has to wonder if composite blades of plastic and ceramic or steel might not soon be seen.

Whatever the outcome of all these lines of research and design, several things are certain. One is that tomorrow's blades will be thinner and sharper thanks to stronger alloys and materials used in blades. This, in turn, may make longer blades practical on both civilian and military combat weapons.

Regardless of the materials used to create these blades, it seems likely that future combat blades will be similar to those of the past since the cutting mechanism of the bowie and similar slashing weapons, as well as the dagger and stiletto stabbing designs, have been perfected for over a century at least and arguably for several millennia. It seems probable that if today's knife owner could see the fighting blade of 3000 A.D., he'd recognize it for what it was, even if it contained a motorized or even computerized system that moved its blade automatically for greater cutting power or unfolded it two or three times along microhinged lines that leave a folding blade longer than its grip. The materials used in its construction may make the blade gossamer-thin, but it will still look much like today's knives.

And tomorrow's combat blades will most likely be just as important to tomorrow's citizen and soldier as they are today: utilitarian tools that can peel an apple, serve as an emergency pry bar, or protect their owners, even if an enemy manages to get to within arm's reach despite massive firepower or if a government tries to disarm its citizens, allowing criminals to prey freely on the helpless.

Some things never change.

Modern Combat Blades: The Best in Edged Weaponry

BLADE IMPORTERS, DEALERS, AND MANUFACTURERS

Al Mar Knives, Inc.
P.O. Box 1626
Lake Oswego, OR 97034
Custom knife maker of the SERE series, Alaskan Bowie, Pathfinder, etc.

Atlanta Cutlery
2143 Gees Mill Rd., Box 839
Conyers, GA 30207
Importer of a wide range of knives, swords, axes, and "exotic" blades as well as a distributer of American knives.

B&D Trading
3935 Fair Hill Rd.
Fair Oaks, CA 95628
Dealer of Executive Edge folder that mimics an ink pen in size and style.

B&T Diversified Industries
1873 93rd Ave.
Indianola, IA 50125
Manufacturer of the Bush Wakker.

Blackjack Knives
Jordan Ave., #D-72
Canoga Park, CA 91303
Manufacturer of Tartan, Blackmoor, Wasp, and a variety of other combat blades.

Bowen Knife Co.
P.O. Box 590
Blackshear, GA 31516
Manufacturer of belt buckle knives.

Brigade Quartermasters
1025 Cobb International Blvd.
Kennesaw, GA 30144-4349
Dealer of several styles of inexpensive machetes, combat knives, and an umbrella sword.

Bud/K/Worldwide
P.O. Box 565
Moultrie, GA 31776
Importer of inexpensive copies of "classic" knives like the Bowie and Arkansas Toothpick.

Camillus Cutlery Co.
52-54 W. Genesee St.
Camillus, NY 13031-0083
Military knife contractor and manufacturer of excellent pocketknives, including multiblade lockbacks.

Catoctin Cutlery
P.O. Box 188, 17 S. Main St.
Smithsburg, MD 21783
Marketer/importer of a wide range of combat-style knives.

Century International Arms, Inc.
P.O. Box 714
St. Albans, VT 05478
Importer of military surplus swords, bayonets, and combat knives.

Cold Steel, Inc.
2128 Knoll Dr., Unit D
Ventura, CA 93003
Manufacturer of combat knives, including Bowies and Tantos.

Collector's Armoury, Inc.
800 Slaters Lane, P.O. Box 1061
Alexandria, VA 22313
Dealer of tempered reproduction swords and new and surplus bayonets and combat knives.

Cutlery Shoppe
5461 Kendall St.
Boise, ID 83706-1248
Importer of foreign knives and dealer for many major American knife manufacturers.

Cutlery World
2841 Hickory Valley Rd.
Chattanooga, TN 37421
Marketer of a wide range of major knife brands, including some special models unavailable elsewhere.

The Dutchman
P.O. Box 12548
Overland Park, KS 66212
Importer of sword canes.

The Edge Company
P.O. Box 826
Brattleboro, VT 05301
Importer of a wide range of folders, pen knives, and combat-style knives.

Ek Commando Knife Co.
Box 6622
Richmond, VA 23230
Manufacturer of combat knives.

Gerber Legendary Blades
14200 SW 72nd St.
Portland, OR 97223
Manufacturer of folders and fixed-blade combat knives.

Great Lakes Distributing
600 W. Orange
Greenville, MI 48838
Importer of the Silver Shadow, designed by Gil Hibben.

Gutmann Cutlery Company, Inc.
900 S. Columbus Ave.
Mt. Vernon, NY 10550
Importer of a wide variety of survival, combat, and folding knives.

Ralph Dewey Harris
P.O. Box 597
Grovetown, GA 30813
Maker of custom knives.

Jantz Supply
222 E. Main
Davis, OK 73030
Supplier of knife-making blades, handle materials, and knifesmithing tools.

Ka-Bar Cutlery, Inc.
5777 Grant Ave.
Cleveland, OH 44105
Manufacturer of Ka-Bar fighting knife.

Kershaw Cutlery Co.
6024 Jean Rd., Suite-D
Lake Oswego, OR 97034
Dealer of lockback folders and survival knives.

H.G. Long & Company
Box 6622
Richmond, VA 23230
Importer of Sheffield cutlery, including the V-42.

Military Replica Arms
P.O. Box 360006
Tampa, FL 33673-0006
Maker of military-style reproduction swords with scabbards.

Steve Mullin/Pack River Knife Co.
500 W. Center Valley Rd.
Sandpoint, ID 83864
Maker of custom knives.

Museum Replicas Limited
2143 Gees Mill Rd., Box 840
Conyers, GA 30207
Dealer of a wide range of historical reproductions of swords, knives, maces, and battle-axes with tempered blades.

Parker Cutlery
6928 Lee Highway, P.O. Box 22668
Chattanooga, TN 37415
Importer of a wide variety of knives.

PL&T Products
P.O. Box 748
Eastpoint, FL 32328
Maker of inexpensive "made in America" military-style combat knives.

Randall Knives
Box 1988
Orlando, FL 32802
Maker of custom-made combat knives that were popular among American troops during World War II, Korea, and Vietnam.

Chris Reeve
6147 Corporal Ln.
Boise, ID 83704
Maker of custom-crafted knives including hollow-handled survival knives made from one piece of steel to prevent breakage.

A.G. Russell
1705 Highway 71 North
Springdale, AR 72764-2397
Maker of custom knives, including One Hand Knife, Combat Master Bowies, and Sting, plus distributor for other major brands of knives.

SARCO, Inc.
323 Union St.
Stirling, NJ 07980
Dealer of military surplus bayonets and combat knives.

The Savage Edge
270 Mendon Rd.
S. Attleboro, MA 02703
Manufacturer of Viking Raider ax and combat knives.

Sherwood International
18714 Parthenia St.
Northridge, CA 91324
Importer of military bayonets and combat knives.

SOG Specialty Knives
P.O. Box 1024
Edmonds, WA 98020
Manufacturer of combat folders and fixed knives, including the SOG Winder I, Air-SOG, Tigershark, etc.

Sportsman's Guide
965 Decatur Ave. N.
Golden Valley MN 55427-4398
Dealer of collector's swords and sporting knives.

Spyderco, Inc.
P.O. Box 800
Golden, CO 80402
Dealer of Clipit folding knives.

Spye Knife Company
P.O. Box 902
Ft. Pierce, FL 34954
Dealer of Ballistic knife modeled after Soviet military knife, along with various accessories, including baton, grappling hook, and spear gun for divers.

Ralph L. Stevens
1298 Som Center Rd., Suite #223
Mayfield, OH 44124
Distributor of Cobra, as well as Shrade and Buck folding knives.

Taylor Cutlery Mfg. Co.
806 E. Center St., P.O. Box 1638
Kingsport, TN 37662
Importer of folders, butterfly, and combat knives.

Tekna Design Group
P.O. Box 849
Belmont, CA 94002
Manufacturer of high-tech skin diving knives using plastic and innovative designs.

Tiffin Family Knife Co.
P.O. Box 748
Eastpoint, FL 32328
Importer of inexpensive combat and reproduction knives; minimum order of $50.

Toledo Armas S.A.
302 Ponce de Leon Blvd.
St. Augustine, FL 32084
Importer of Spanish-made knives.

United Cutlery Corp.
1425 United Blvd.
Sevierville, TN 37862
Importer of inexpensive imported knives, including lockbacks and combat knives.

Valor Corporation
5555 NW 36th Ave.
Miami, FL 33142
Importer of lockback folders and combat-style knives.

Westbury Sales Co.
156 Post Ave.
Westbury, NY 11590
Importer of inexpensive folders and combat knives.

Y.B. Technology
P.O. Box 65 Snowdon Station
Montreal, Quebec, CANADA H3X 3T3
Manufacturer of One Arm Bandit for single-hand opening of folding knives.

Appendix B
PUBLICATIONS AND VIDEOS

BOOKS ABOUT COMBAT BLADES

Blade Master: Advanced Survival Skills for the Knife Fighter
by John Sanchez
Paladin Press
P.O. Box 1307
Boulder, CO 80306

Bloody Iron
by Jenks and Brown
Paladin Press
P.O. Box 1307
Boulder, CO 80306

The Book of the Sword
by Richard F. Burton
Dover Publications, Inc.
31 East 2nd St.
Mineola, NY 11501

Commando Dagger: The Complete Illustrated History of the Fairbairn-Sykes Fighting Knife
by Leroy Thompson
Paladin Press
P.O. Box 1307
Boulder, CO 80306

The Complete Bladesmith: Forging Your Way to Perfection
by Jim Hrisoulas
Paladin Press
P.O. Box 1307
Boulder, CO 80306

Field Knife Evaluations: The Good, the Bad, and the Ugly of Hard-Use Knives
by Jerry Younkins
Paladin Press
P.O. Box 1307
Boulder, CO 80306

Hidden Threat: A Guide to Covert Weapons
by Mark Smith
Paladin Press
P.O. Box 1307
Boulder, CO 80306

An Introduction to Switchblade Knives
by Ben Myers and Lowell Myers, JD
American Eagle Publishing
P.O. Box 4341
Chicago, IL 60680

Knives (annual editions)
Edited by Ken Warner
DBI Books, Inc.
4092 Commercial Ave.
Northbrook, IL 60062

Knives and the Law: Dirks, Daggers, and Dangerous Knives
by James R. Nielsen
Knife World Publications
730 Broadway
Knoxville, TN 37917

Knives, Knife Fighting & Related Hassles: How to Survive a Real Knife Fight
by Marc "Animal" MacYoung
Paladin Press
P.O. Box 1307
Boulder, CO 80306

The Master Bladesmith: Advanced Studies in Steel
by Jim Hrisoulas
Paladin Press
P.O. Box 1307
Boulder, CO 80306

Modern American Fighting Knives
by Robert S. McKay
Unique Publications
4201 Vanowen Place
Burbank, CA 91505

Pool Cues, Beer Bottles, & Baseball Bats: Animal's Guide to Improvised Weapons for Self-Defense and Survival
by Marc "Animal" MacYoung
Paladin Press
P.O. Box 1307
Boulder, CO 80306

Put 'em Down, Take 'em Out! Knife Fighting Techniques from Folsom Prison
by Don Pentecost
Paladin Press
P.O. Box 1307
Boulder, CO 80306

Slash & Thrust
by John Sanchez
Paladin Press
P.O. Box 1307
Boulder, CO 80306

Survival/Fighting Knives
by Leroy Thompson
Paladin Press
P.O. Box 1307
Boulder, CO 80306

Switchblade: The Ace of Blades
by Ragnar Benson
Paladin Press
P.O. Box 1307
Boulder, CO 80306

U.S. Military Knives, Books I–IV
by M.H. Cole
501 Ridge Rd.
Birmingham, AL 35206

MAGAZINES ABOUT COMBAT BLADES

Blade
P.O. Box 22007
Chattanooga, TN 37422

Knife World
P.O. Box 3395
Knoxville, TN 37927

VIDEOS ABOUT KNIFE COMBAT

Defending Against the Blade
Paladin Press
P.O. Box 1307
Boulder, CO 80306

Surviving Edged Weapons
Calibre Press
666 Dundee Rd., Ste. 1607
Northbrook, IL 60062